Truly Human/Truly Divine

D1227542

Truly Human/Truly Divine

Christological Language and the Gospel Form

M. Eugene Boring

CBP Press
St. Louis, Missouri

© 1984 CBP Press

All rights reserved. No part of this book may be reproduced by any method without the publisher's written permission. Address: CBP Press, Box 179, St. Louis, MO 63166.

Library of Congress Cataloging in Publication Data

Boring, M. Eugene.
  Truly human/truly divine.

  Bibliography: p.
  1. Bible. N.T. Gospels—Criticism, interpretations, etc. 2. Jesus Christ—Person and offices. 3. Jesus Christ—Divinity. 4. Jesus Christ—Humanity. I. Title.
BS2555.2.B64 1984   232′.8   84-11382
ISBN 0-8272-3625-5

All scripture quotations, unless otherwise indicated, are from the Revised Standard Version of the Bible, copyrighted 1946, 1952, 1971, 1973.

Manufactured in the United States of America

Contents

Preface: Claims and Disclaimers

This book has a modest goal: to help "ordinary" Christian people to talk about the Jesus of the Gospels more faithfully. The "ordinary" Christians I have in mind—students, pastors, church school teachers, church members who want to articulate a faith that is intellectually honest—are in fact an extraordinary company, the mainstay of the church's life and mission. But they are not specialists in biblical study, theology, or the philosophy of language.

This book is not written for specialists. Should a copy fall into the hands of an occasional Bible scholar, professional theologian, logician, or philosopher of language, he or she will recognize numerous instances where I have not supplied the documentation, nuances, and qualifications customary in scholarly discussions. As I am presently at work on a more technical treatment of this subject, I consider this simplified treatment something of a trial balloon for the larger work, and invite critique and suggestions.

This book is written mainly for "insiders," understood entirely in a non-smug manner. That is, it is addressed primarily to those persons within the community of faith who have long heard both the language of divinity and the language of humanity used with reference to Jesus, and who affirm it at least in some degree, but who aren't sure what to make of it. But I would be very pleased should this small book come to the attention of a few of those inquiring "outsiders," that rather large group of thoughtful, serious, searching people who are attracted to the Christian faith but suppose they are turned off to it because of its talk of miracles, the divinity of Jesus, and such, and are uninterested in making a commitment which seems to call for a surrender of intellectual integrity.

This book is concerned with only a narrow spectrum of our Christian life, namely, how we think and talk about Christ; i.e., it is concerned with Christology. It does not attempt to discuss everything we should know about Jesus or the meaning of being a Christian. Thinking and talking are not everything, or even the main thing. Following Jesus, living a life that corresponds to our faith, is far more important. But how we talk and think about Christ is important, and affects how, or even whether, we follow.

This book is aimed at helping our talk about Christ to be more faithful. This means being more faithful to the Bible. Christian theology is not a speculative discipline but the exposition of the meaning of a document, or collection of documents—the Scriptures of the Old and New Testaments, which are normative for Christian faith. Christian talk of Jesus must be faithful to the Bible, and that means faithfulness to what we find it to be in the process of careful, critical study. Christian talk of Jesus must be faithful to the church and its classical statements of the faith found in the early creedal declarations. We are not the first to attempt to be both faithful and honest in our talk of Jesus. We stand in a great tradition and must be responsible to it even when we don't simply repeat it. And Christian talk of Jesus must be faithful to ourselves and our contemporary world, which is also God's world. This book attempts to articulate, in a simple manner, a way of thinking and talking about the Jesus in the Gospels that is faithful to the Bible, to the classical Christian confessions, and to ourselves and our world.

This book was written with much help from family, colleagues, brothers and sisters in the church, and friends. The dedication to my family attempts to indicate something of what I owe them for their contribution, mostly indirect, to what I have been able to learn about the actual divine/human subject matter with which this book is concerned. Those who have helped, directly or indirectly, with its actual writing are those groups with which I have shared, in various preliminary forms, some of the contents of this book as lectures: First Christian Church, Alva, Oklahoma; First Christian Church, Paris, Tennessee; First Christian Church, Liberal, Kansas; students and faculty at the Graduate Seminary, Phillips University (Seminary Series Lectures, 1981); students, faculty, and ministers at Bethany College (Scott Lectures, Ministers' Week, 1984); and those colleagues and friends who have read the manuscript at various stages and offered helpful suggestions: Joe R. Jones, James F. Caton, Harold E. Hatt, Herbert H. Lambert, Susan Schreiner, G. Ervin Crain, Werner Kelber, Fred B. Craddock, Ronald E. Osborn, and Stan Duncan. I am grateful for the help in preparing the final form of this book provided by Raymond F. Person, Jr., my student assistant, and Julia Grossman, faculty secretary, two extraordinarily capable people whose assistance has extended far beyond the mechanical and the line of duty.

To my parents,
Mr. and Mrs. Maynard Boring,
Who nurtured me in the faith
Of the one true God.

To my children,
Bonnie, Brad, and Beth,
Who have taught me much
About true humanity.

1

The Gospel as the Power of God

The Issue
Faith in Christ and Belief in Miracles
"Divine Men" in Mark's World
Mark as Interpreter of the Miracle Stories
Epiphany Christology in the Miracle Stories
The Problem with a "Divine Man" Jesus

The Issue

In the crucial scene in the Gospel of Mark, the religious leaders taunt Jesus with these words: "Let the Christ, the King of Israel, come down now from the cross, that we may see and believe" (Mark 15:32).

Well, could he have done it? Obviously, he *did not* do it; he died in a surprisingly short period of time (15:44). But the initial question for understanding Mark's presentation of the meaning of Christ is raised by the text of the Gospel itself: Could Jesus have come down from the cross? The question may seem crude; merely to raise it seems in bad taste. But crucifixions are crude, and the New Testament is not too polite to avoid either the cross or the questions it poses.

Some Christian readers of the Gospel of Mark, sincere and logical, will answer with a quick "yes": if he could walk on the water, he could come down from the cross.

Others, equally sincere and equally logical, will answer just as quickly with a "no." Can a superman who can come down from the cross be said to die a human death at all? At the center of our faith stands the affirmation that the Jesus who had lived among us truly died with and for us. When both a simple "yes" and "no" are problematic in answer to a question, we need to look more closely at the question.

Actually, there are two questions here, which we must be careful to distinguish even if we don't separate. The first question has to do with the "real" historical Jesus of Nazareth, the actual person who was crucified in A.D. 30. Perhaps most people would assume that the question applies exclusively to this person. What "other" Jesus is there? The second question applies to Jesus as he is presented in the Gospel of Mark, about A.D. 70, the Jesus who is the subject of the faith and preaching of Mark's church. This second question refers to the Jesus whom the Markan text intends for us to see in the particular way this Gospel presents him. We may call the first of these "the historical Jesus" (A.D. 30) and the second "the Markan Jesus" (A.D. 70). Of course, these two are related, but are they identical? Even if for many readers these two may be virtually identical, it is still important to distinguish them, and to know which we are talking about.

We are ultimately interested, of course, in the historical Jesus, the actual person of the man of Nazareth. Christian faith has never believed that we are saved by a figure who was crucified only in a story. But we can talk about the historical person only after it has become clear to us how he is presented to us in the documents preserved for us by the early church, principally the four Gospels in the New Testament. Before we can make statements about the historical Jesus, we must first be interested in the Jesus of the Gospels, recognizing that even here he may not always be presented in the same way. (Otherwise, why *four*?) So in the following, unless otherwise stated, "Jesus" refers to Jesus as the Gospel of Mark presents him. Our question is thus whether Mark intends for us to believe, on the basis of his Gospel, that the figure on the cross could have descended from it if he had so desired.

This is not a speculative question posited on the basis of some perverse curiosity or lust for sensationalism. What is at stake is a way of thinking about Jesus, the meaning of who he is (was?) and how (if at all?) he represents God. That is, a *Christological* issue is raised by this question.

The logic of the chief priests' taunt is clear. If Jesus is the Christ, then he is not an ordinary human being, but a being filled with divine power, the "Son of God." Mark has made it clear to the reader in 14:61 that the chief priests in the story, like the Christians in Mark's church, identify the "Christ" and the "Son of God." ("Son of the Blessed" indicates the Jewish hesitation to pronounce the word "God," but of course means the same as "Son of God.") The assumption in the chief priests' taunt is that the Christ is not an "ordinary" human being, but a being filled with divine power, a "divine being." If he is the Christ, he should be able to come down from the cross. Was he able to do so?

There is much in what Mark has already told the reader that seems to demand an affirmative answer to this question. The picture of Jesus as "Strong Son of God" permeates the Markan narrative, as it does the Christian tradition as a whole. This is a picture of a mighty superhuman Christ who, it would seem, must have remained on the cross for some other reason than that he was not *able* to come down. Our preliminary diagram of the chief priests' logic thus appears as follows:

Diagram 1

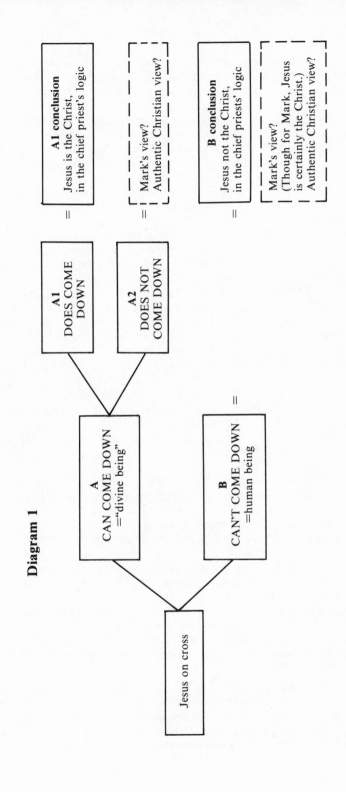

A1 conclusion
Jesus is the Christ,
in the chief priest's logic

Mark's view?
Authentic Christian view?

B conclusion
Jesus not the Christ,
in the chief priests' logic

Mark's view?
(Though for Mark, Jesus
is certainly the Christ.)
Authentic Christian view?

A1
DOES COME
DOWN

A2
DOES NOT
COME DOWN

A
CAN COME DOWN
="divine being"

B
CAN'T COME DOWN
=human being

Jesus on cross

Let us briefly review some of the evidence in Mark which seems to indicate that he shares the logic of the chief priests, a logic which presupposes that if Jesus were in *fact* the Christ, he *could* descend from the cross:

(1:7-8) In Mark, the strange wilderness preacher called John the Baptist has just one message: he announces the coming of "the Mighty One," who will baptize with the Holy Spirit. Although John does not name this "Mighty One," the early church and Mark certainly understood him to be speaking of Jesus. The first person in the story to say anything about Jesus at all is this true prophet of God, who introduces Jesus to the reader of Mark as one whose dominant characteristic is that he is filled with the mighty power of God.

(1:9-11) This understanding of Jesus is immediately confirmed by the story of Jesus' baptism. A voice from heaven announces (to Jesus and the reader) that Jesus is indeed the Son of God, and the Spirit of God descends into him (this is a more accurate translation of *eis auton* in 1:10, and is what Mark characteristically means by the phrase). The modern reader is apt to be misled by the "soft" connotations we associate with key words in this text ("dove," "spirit"), so that he might miss what Mark intends to portray as an almost violent infusion of divine power into Jesus. In biblical usage, the word "spirit," when it refers to the Spirit of God, means "power," superhuman divine power (examples: Judges 14:6, 19; 15:14; 1 Samuel 11:6; 1 Kings 18:12; 2 Kings 2:15-16; Isaiah 11:2-4; 31:3; Ezekiel 37:1-14; Matthew 12:28; Luke 1:17; 4:14; Acts 1:8; 8:39; 10:38; Romans 15:19; 1 Corinthians 2:4; 2 Timothy 1:7). That this is the right connotation here is clear from 1:12, where the Spirit which has just descended into Jesus "throws him out" into the wilderness (the RSV phrase "drove him out" is *ekballei,* the same Greek word used by Mark when Jesus violently casts unholy spirits out of others in 1:34; 1:39; 3:22, etc.).

(1:13) Jesus was tested forty days by Satan. In Mark, this was entirely a test of the newly given power of Jesus, not a "temptation" in the moral sense, as in Matthew 4:1-11 and Luke 4:1-13. In Mark, the power-filled Son of God meets the power of Satan in a portentous test of strength, and he emerges victorious. As Mark later lets Jesus explain it (3:27), he has "bound" the "strong man" and is now "plundering his house." Jesus, "Strong Son of God," emerges triumphant from the wilderness and begins to stride through Galilee undoing the work of Satan by the mighty divine power with which he is filled.

He casts out demons (1:21-28; 1:39; 3:22; 5:1-20; 7:24-30; 9:14-29) and even gives his disciples power to do this (6:7; 9:38).

He heals the sick (1:29-34; 1:40-45; 2:1-12; 3:1-6; 3:10; 5:25-34; 6:56; 7:31-37; 8:22-26; 10:46-52), sometimes merely by their touching the edge of his robe (5:28-29; 6:56).

He is not subject to the laws of nature which would destroy others, but calms the storm on the lake of Galilee with a word (4:35-41) and walks on the water to the disciples' boat in the middle of the lake (6:45-52).

He predicts his own death as something within his own divine power, and announces in advance that he will arise from the dead (8:31; 9:31; 10:33-34).

Jesus' resurrection is usually spoken of in the New Testament as the act of *God*, so that if Jesus is the subject, the verb is in the passive voice (e.g. Matthew 16:21; 17:9, 23; 20:19; 26:32; 28:6; Luke 9:22; 24:6; John 2:22; 21:14; Romans 4:25; 6:4, 9; 8:34; 1 Corinthians 15:4, 12, 13, 14, 16, 17, 20; 1 Thessalonians 1:10; 2 Timothy 2:8); however, here Jesus consistently speaks of "rising" (active voice) as though it were something in his own power. This is what Mark intends the reader to understand, for in each of these predictions of his resurrection, Jesus speaks of himself as the "Son of Man." Contrary to initial appearances, this strange title which only Jesus uses of himself does not mean simply "human being," but refers to the *heavenly* apocalyptic figure who was expected to come at the end in power and glory to judge the world as God's representative (Daniel 7:13-14, Matthew 25:21-46). Thus, when Jesus speaks of himself as "Son of Man" in Mark, this would to the ancient reader be a claim to divine power, not a confession of human weakness. The Son of Man is the one who can rise from the dead by his own power, and indeed is able to raise the dead during his earthly life (5:21-43).

Although we have far from exhausted the possible Markan references to Jesus' power, we have seen enough to acknowledge that Mark does present Jesus as a superhumanly powerful figure. The typical word for Jesus' miracles is not the usual Hellenistic word, *thauma* ("amazing thing"), or *semeion* or *teras*, used elsewhere in the New Testament for Jesus' miracles, but *dunamis* ("mighty deed"), related to our words "dynamite," "dynamo." It is characteristic of Jesus that power goes forth from him, almost involuntarily (5:30). The unbelieving judgment of the religious leaders at the crucifixion, that Jesus was *not able* to come down from the cross, would thus seem to be negated by anyone who believes Mark's presentation of Jesus as the powerful Son of God. (The chief priests' "He *cannot* save himself" in 15:31 uses the verb form *dunamai*, "to be able," for which *dunamis* is the noun.) If the unbelievers respond to Jesus' cross by saying "He is not able to come down," it would seem that the believing response would be to affirm "He is able to come down," locating Mark's view at point A2 in Diagram 1. But is this Mark's intent? Is this an authentic Christian understanding of the meaning of Jesus as Son of God? We have not settled this question, but before we continue with it, we need to clarify just what we should understand by Mark's presentation of this miracle-working superman from Nazareth.

Faith in Christ and Belief in Miracles

The problem which Mark has intentionally presented, and which comes to sharpest focus in the chief priests' taunt at the cross, is the relation of believing in miracles to believing in Jesus as the Christ. The chief priests' position is clear: *If* they could believe in some stupendous miracle done by Jesus, *then* they would, they claim, believe in him as the Christ. "Let the Christ, the King of Israel, come down now from the cross, that we may see and believe" (15:32).

Before we continue this discussion, I need to address two particular types of readers, readers of both Mark and these pages. The first type is the one who has no trouble believing in miracles, or at least is able to acknowledge that the historical Jesus did the kind of miracles which Mark attributes to him. To this reader, the issue seems to be simple: Disbelieve (miracles and Jesus) with the chief priests, or believe (miracles and Jesus) with Mark. This reader shares the logic of the chief priests: If he was the Christ he was able to perform amazing miracles and could have come down from the cross. The fact that he did not do so is explained in terms of a theory of the atonement which requires that Jesus die as a sacrifice for human sin or as a demonstration of his love. We shall come back to this theory later. For the moment, we need to note that this reader shares the logic of the chief priests (which may come as a surprise to him or her), and disagrees with them on only the major premise: whether Jesus could have performed such an amazing stunt. Such a reader supposes that this was also Mark's own logic, since Mark certainly believes in Jesus as the Christ, and since he presents Jesus as demonstrating the power of God at work within him by performing many miracles. Mark too, it is supposed, must have believed, and wants the faithful reader to believe, that Jesus *could* have come down from the cross. Such a reader will be tempted to locate Mark's logic, and his own, at point A2 in the diagram.

But there is another reader, who may have followed this discussion and the narrative in Mark with less patience than the first reader. This second type of reader has difficulty believing in miracles at all, those of Jesus or anyone else. Such a reader is aware that miracle stories have been told about great figures in all ages, have been believed by the superstitious, pre- or unscientific, or just plain gullible of every generation. His objections may have to do with the uniformity of the cause-effect nexus of natural law in which he believes the world exists, or his objections may be of a moral nature—miracles do raise questions of ethics and not just of physics. In any case, multitudes of readers of Mark (who are mostly, in fact, nonreaders, having given up on the Bible and being acquainted with the Bible's witness to Jesus only secondhand) have objections (philosophical, historical, and ethical) to believing in a Jesus who walks on water, withers fig trees with a curse, feeds five thousand people with a boy's lunch, and goes through the charade of being crucified, knowing all along that he could miraculously call it off any time he wanted to. If *this* reader accepts the logic of the chief priests, and the purported logic of Mark, he seems to be shut out from Christian faith, at least as Mark defines it: no faith in a miracle-working Jesus, no Christian faith. This reader has two choices: to accept the judgment of the first reader that he cannot be a Christian or, if he is attracted to Christianity anyway or has inherited it, and wishes to persist in trying to be a Christian, to suppose that he must do this in non-biblical terms. This reader typically turns the Bible over to those whom he condescendingly regards as literalists, and works out some kind of Christian faith based on the supposed ethical teaching of Jesus, the ideal of love, the self-discovery of his human potential, etc.

16

Diagram 2

Two Lines of Inference
(Both Within the Logic of the Chief Priests)

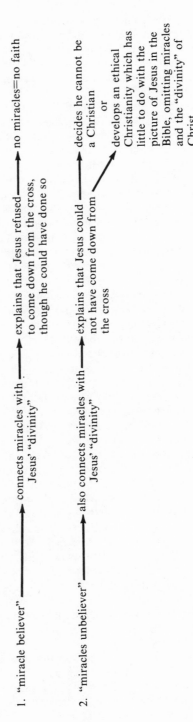

1. "miracle believer" → connects miracles with Jesus' "divinity" → explains that Jesus refused to come down from the cross, though he could have done so → no miracles=no faith

2. "miracles unbeliever" → also connects miracles with Jesus' "divinity" → explains that Jesus could not have come down from the cross → decides he cannot be a Christian

    or

    develops an ethical Christianity which has little to do with the picture of Jesus in the Bible, omitting miracles and the "divinity" of Christ

Two lines of inference are represented here. Neither may seem very attractive. Are these the only alternatives? Does either represent Mark's way of thinking about Jesus? The one reader may suppose that he "believes" in Jesus as the Christ because he accepts miracles; the other may suppose that he must reject the faith, at least in its biblical form, because he can only regard the crucified one as sharing our human weakness, victimized by the pretensions of religion and the expediency of politics, but helpless like the rest of us once he has been crucified by them. The first reader may say that he believes in the "divinity" of Jesus, the second that he affirms Jesus' "humanity." Both of these points of view are locked into the perspective of the chief priests, disagreeing only on whether Jesus could have "done it," but sharing the same logic, the same *way* of thinking about Jesus as those who put him to death. They both tend to suppose that they share Mark's perspective as well. But before either of them draws this conclusion, we need to look more closely at just what Mark intends by presenting Jesus as a miracle-working superhuman figure.

We should first quickly notice a few passages which Mark has sprinkled among the miracle stories to give the reader the clue that he himself does not accept the simple logic that if-Jesus-was-the-Christ-then-he-must-have-been-able-to-work-miracles-including-come-down-from-the-cross, nor the reversal of this equation, that if-Jesus-worked-miracles-then-he-must-be-the-Christ. Mark calls in question the identification "Christ=miracle worker" from both sides of the equation.

In 3:20, the Jerusalem scribes do not question that he casts out demons, but rather than coming to faith in him as the Christ, they accuse him of being in league with the devil. In 6:2, the hometown folk of Nazareth do not question that he does "mighty works," but rather than becoming disciples, they are scandalized by him. Mark here specifically connects faith in "mighty works" (6:2) and "unbelief" (6:6), just as he declares that although Jesus was the Christ, "he *was not able (dunamai!)* to do any mighty work *(dunamis!)* there" because of their unbelief (6:5). This theme is developed in the Passion story, 14:1ff, and will be discussed below. In 6:14-16 Herod Antipas, petty ruler of Galilee at the pleasure of Rome, hears of Jesus' miracles, believes them, and has an explanation for them: Jesus is John the Baptist who has been raised from the dead! But Herod is hardly thereby made into a Christian in Mark's eyes, regardless of how many miracles and resurrections he may believe. And in 13:22 Jesus makes it clear that false prophets and false Christs will work their miracles, but are nonetheless false. So, although Mark presents Jesus as both miracle worker and Christ, from a number of directions he is at pains to disallow both the inference "If miracle-worker, therefore Christ" and its supposed corollary, "If Christ, therefore miracle-worker." This should be disquieting both to the miracle-believing and the miracle-rejecting believers in Jesus' "divinity" and his "humanity" respectively.

If Mark does not fit the pattern of the chief priests' logic, what *does* he want to say by presenting Jesus as a divine wonder-worker? Before proceeding, we need two items of information, one about Mark's world, the other about Mark's writing, which will lead us within hearing distance of the message of the miracle stories.

The "Divine Man" in Mark's World

We must to some extent understand Mark before either our "yes" or our "no" to the gospel he declares makes much sense. But if either miracle-believer or miracle-denier is to understand Mark, such a reader must think his or her way back into the world in which Mark's Gospel was written and to which it was addressed, a world which in regard to miracles was a very different world than ours. Not that everyone in that supposedly "primitive" age believed in miracles, for not everyone did. But the average citizen of the first-century Hellenistic world was acquainted with a typical figure of that world which, for the sake of convenience, we will call the "divine man" *(theios aner,* plural *theioi andres).* This does not mean that everyone in the first-century world knew a "divine man" personally, or that they were neighborhood figures, but that "divine men" were a part of the life-world of the ordinary first-century Hellenistic citizen whether he had seen one or not, just as moon rockets and computers are part of our life-world whether we have personal contact with them or not. The figure of the "divine man" was already there in the person's mind, because this figure was a part of his culture, and perhaps a part of his personal experience, before he had ever heard of Jesus, the church, or the Christian faith. This fact is very important for understanding the Gospel of Mark and much of the New Testament. Who were these "divine men"?

By using the term "divine man," I do not mean to imply that there necessarily was a fixed, uniform conception or a rigidly defined sociological type known in the ancient world as "divine man" or "son of God." The term "divine man" itself was only occasionally used, and only incidentally equated with "son of God." But the figure it has come to designate in recent discussions was a common figure, both in the culture and in the literature. I use "divine man" as a convenient technical term of much current New Testament scholarship to refer to that figure in the Hellenistic world, including Judaism, who was not subject to the limitations of human finite existence because his life was a manifestation of the divine power. The "divine man," whether labeled with this designation or not, was that figure who was more than human but less than a god, who could accomplish amazing supernatural feats of wisdom, healing, and exorcism, and could overcome such physical dangers as storms, by virtue of the divine power at work in him.

Sometimes this figure was understood to be not a human being at all, but a god in human disguise (cf. Ovid, *Metamorphoses* 8.620ff., Acts 14:11; 28:6). But more often, a semi-divine, semi-human borderline figure is thought of. For instance, Philo, a Hellenistic Jew of Alexandria in Egypt and a contemporary of Jesus, describes a *theios aner* (apparently referring to Moses) as "neither God nor man, but . . . on the borderline between the uncreated and the perishing form of being" (*Som.* II, 234). In the Hellenistic age, contemporary figures were understood in "divine man" categories, and older heroes from tradition and legend were reinterpreted in "divine man" terms. Thus the life of Pythagoras of the sixth century B.C.

is retold in the second and third centuries A.D. as the story of a "divine man," and Philo's first-century "Life of Moses" enhances the traditional image of Moses with some "divine man" features. It was in the air.

The *theios aner* was frequently of divine ancestry or parentage, or born in some marvelous way (such as Alexander the Great, Hercules, Moses as retold in Philo). His childhood was often full of extraordinary wonders (Pythagoras, Moses in Philo). His adult life was characterized by healings, exorcisms, and supernatural knowledge of mysteries and the future, as well as miracles of nature, showing that the divine power was present in him (Asclepius, Pythagoras, Alexander the Great, Rabbi Chanina ben Dosa, Dionysus). The accounts of the "death" or disappearance from the earth of such "divine men" are usually vague and ambiguous (Philo's "Life of Moses," Pythagoras, Hercules), for there is obviously a problem in narrating the death of one who, though not quite a god, is not quite human either.

No secondary account of these figures as they appeared in the Hellenistic world and its literature can substitute for a reading of the primary sources themselves. Fortunately, these have been collected and are readily available; the reader is encouraged to examine the accounts of miracle workers typical of the world in which the New Testament was written. (See the anthologies assembled by David R. Cartlidge and David L. Dungan, and by Moses Hadas and Morton Smith listed in the bibliography at the end of this chapter.)

Much of what we are interested in seeing is illustrated in the "Life of Apollonius of Tyana" written by Philostratus near the end of the second century A.D.[1] Apollonius lived about the same time as Jesus of Nazareth, being born around 20 B.C. He grew up near the hometown of Paul, Tarsus in Cilicia, and spent his adult life traveling over much of the Mediterranean world. We do not know just what the "historical Apollonius" was like, but in the retelling of his life story by Philostratus, he appears as the typical "divine man." Amid miraculous signs, he was born in a meadow after the Egyptian God Proteus had appeared to his mother and announced that the child to be born to her would be divine. Apollonius was a precocious child who spoke pure Attic Greek, "not influenced by the barbarian speech of the Cappadocians." He understood all languages, though he never studied any. As he traveled around he healed many sick people, cast out demons, and raised the dead.

After Apollonius had become famous, the Emperor Domitian resolved to destroy him. Of his own accord, Apollonius allowed himself to be arrested and tried in Domitian's court. However, he confided to his disciples, "I myself know more than mere men do, for I know all things . . . and that I have not come to Rome on behalf of the foolish will become perfectly clear; for *I myself am in no danger with respect to my own body nor will I be killed by this tyrant*" (VII, 14). During his trial, he removes his shackles at will. After hearing Apollonius' defense, Domitian declares that he will not condemn him. But Apollonius considers this a ruse, and responds: "Give me my freedom, if you will, but if not, then send someone to imprison my body, for it is impossible to imprison my soul! Indeed, you will not even take my body, for [quoting Homer, *Iliad* 22:13] 'you cannot kill me since I am not a mortal man,'" and, saying this, he vanished from the courtroom, suddenly appearing to his disciple Damis and a friend in another town (VIII, 5). [Could Apollonius have "come down from the cross"?]

Philostratus relates various conflicting accounts of the supposed "death" of Apollonius, attaching the most credence to those stories in which he enters the temple of one of the gods and just disappears, amid the chorus of heavenly choirs singing "Come up from earth, come to heaven, come."

Stories of such figures, and sometimes a personal encounter with a traveling miracle-worker himself, were a familiar part of the lives and world of those early Christians who first interpreted the significance of Jesus and who finally wrote the New Testament documents.

Mark as Interpreter of the Miracle Stories

The second informational item prerequisite to understanding Mark has to do with the process by which he composes his document and the nature of the resulting composition. Mark is not a reporter who is concerned with "just reporting the facts" objectively as they happened. He was not an eyewitness of the ministry of Jesus, nor is he simply a reporter of the sermons of Peter. The disciplines of form criticism and tradition criticism, as used by New Testament scholars for the past three generations, have made it clear that Mark gets his material from the Christian tradition, that body of material from and about Jesus which was handed down orally in various settings in the church's life (worship, teaching, polemics, missionary preaching, etc.) during the period from Jesus' death (A.D. 30) to the writing of the first Gospel, Mark (A.D. 70). This tradition was not handed down in a body, as one connected corpus, but as a multitude of stories and sayings, each of which was an individual unit with its own point and meaning. Each unit was preserved not because of biographical or historical interest but because in some way it served the needs of the church in preaching, teaching, or celebrating the significance of God's act in Jesus. Each story was a "gospel in miniature," complete in itself. We may think of them as a large group of unstrung beads, each with its own way of witnessing to the gospel as a whole, the good news of what God has done in Jesus.

Mark writes as an interpreter of this tradition. He was apparently the first—certainly the first we know of—Christian to bring a large number of these units together into a connected narrative which included the story of Jesus' death.[2] (An earlier collection, now lost, called by its abbreviation "Q," from the German word for source, *Quelle,* was composed mostly of sayings of Jesus with a minimum of narrative and no story of Jesus' death and resurrection.) Mark composed his Gospel not as a mere collector or editor but as a theologian and author. Mark interpreted his materials, instead of simply repeating them, so that they would address the particular needs of his situation. He did this by his selection and arrangement of the traditional units, and by his editorial modifications and additions to them, as well as by his own composition. The study of this process and its significance for understanding the message of the text composed by Mark is called "redaction criticism" and/or "literary criticism."

It is difficult for us precisely to illustrate this for the person not experienced in the subtleties of redaction criticism, because we have none of Mark's sources independently of their preservation in Mark. We can easily see the same process at work, however, in Matthew and Luke, both of whom later took up Mark as part of their own tradition, included major parts of Mark in their Gospels, and made the same kind of editorial selections, modifications, and additions for their situations which we posit Mark to have made for his. This can be seen in practically every paragraph ("pericope") where Matthew and/or Luke is parallel to Mark, but some clear examples are Mark 8:27-30/Matthew 16:13-20/Luke 9:18-21 and Mark 1:2-11/Matthew 3:1-17/Luke 3:1-22.

Patient, detailed studies of the Gospels have recently enabled us to see that the Gospels should be seen neither as a flat-surface report or composition by a single author who was either simply reporting events as they happened, as a reporter must, nor as compositions by one who was free to compose and invent as a writer of a novel might. The text of the Gospels, to be appreciated aright, must be seen "in depth," as the complex product of the interaction of Jesus himself, his impact on the church and its faith in him as the Christ, and the evangelist-author's own composition. It has thus become common among Bible scholars of all persuasions except the most naively fundamentalistic to distinguish three levels of Gospel materials: (1) "Jesus," (2) "the tradition" (or "the church"), and (3) "the evangelist." These correspond roughly to the dates "30" (Jesus), "30-70" (tradition, for which "50" may serve as a convenient symbolic date), and "70" (for Mark, "90" being a commonly accepted general date for Matthew, Luke, and John).

In actual practice, of course, we must begin with the Gospel materials, and work backward to their sources and finally to our reconstruction of the A.D. 30 events in the life of the historical Jesus. I here present only the generally agreed upon results of this investigation, beginning from A.D. 30. Any assertions about "what actually happened" in the actual history of Jesus are hypothetical and provisional, of course, since we have only indirect sources for the life of Jesus, and these all differ from each other in ways that are very significant for reconstructing the history of Jesus, for they were not written for that purpose but to bear witness to the significance of Jesus for faith. Nonetheless, we are not so ignorant of "what actually happened" in Jesus' life, and what his message actually was, as is sometimes supposed.

On the point we are now considering, the miraculous or nonmiraculous nature of Jesus' life and ministry, there is practically unanimous agreement. Virtually all reconstructions of Jesus' life agree that he appeared among his contemporaries as a miracle worker (healer) and exorcist, though this was not his most characteristic feature. His proclamation of the coming kingdom of God and his consort with "publicans and sinners" distinguished him from others, but even the most skeptical historians concur that people went away from Jesus' presence believing that they had been healed, and

Diagram 3

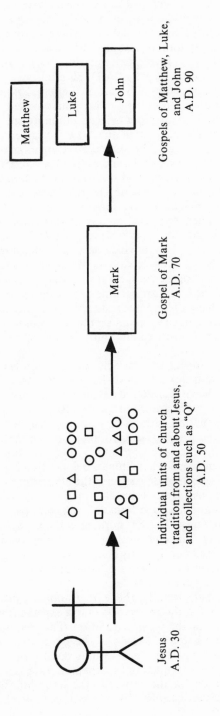

Jesus
A.D. 30

Individual units of church
tradition from and about Jesus,
and collections such as "Q"
A.D. 50

Gospel of Mark
A.D. 70

Gospels of Matthew, Luke,
and John
A.D. 90

Matthew

Luke

John

Mark

23

that evil spirits had been cast out of them. Jesus and his earliest disciples regarded these as preliminary signs of the coming Kingdom, not as proofs of Jesus' "divinity." Such miracles did not separate him from humanity any more than did the similar healings and exorcisms done by Old Testament prophets and New Testament apostles. Such "mighty acts" were one characteristic feature of Jesus' A.D. 30 ministry.

After Easter, this point of contact in the actual life of Jesus opened up the way for the elaboration of the miraculous element in the story of Jesus, making the miraculous more evident and more spectacular. (We can still see this process going on in the New Testament, for instance in the Matthean elaboration of the miraculous element in Mark. Compare Mark 1:32-34 with Matthew 8:16-17 and Mark 10:46-52 with Matthew 20:29-34.) Although amazing events had occurred in the actual life of Jesus, in the church's tradition Jesus became a more miraculous figure than the Jesus of A.D. 30 had been. Old miracle stories were made more miraculous and new ones were applied to Jesus. It was at this stage of the tradition, it is generally believed, that the "nature miracles" were attributed to Jesus. Stories were told of him in which he is not subject to the natural world as other human beings are (walking on the water, stilling the storm, etc.). The ready-made form of the "miracle story" which was already present in both Jewish and Gentile culture became one of the vehicles for preserving and transmitting the stories about Jesus, with the result that the picture of Jesus in the tradition tended more and more to resemble that of the Hellenistic miracle workers whose exploits had originally generated the miracle-story form.

Something happens to a miracle story when it is circulated in isolation from the life and death of Jesus as a whole, as an independent unit of tradition, or when it is clustered only with other miracle stories. In the A.D. 30 setting of the life and message of Jesus, the healings and exorcisms served in conjunction with his message and manner of life in general as a testimony to the presence of God, that God's kingship was breaking into the world in the message and ministry of Jesus; but this did not separate Jesus as a man from other human beings. But a miracle story taken in isolation, as itself a representation of the life and person of Jesus as a whole, shifts the emphasis from Jesus as a man through whom God worked to Jesus as a nonhuman, superhuman being, who has little in common with the rest of humanity. There is nothing in the miracle story itself to affirm Jesus' humanity. The end result of this process, which did not take very long in some circles of the early church, was that Jesus in the tradition took on the features of the Hellenistic "divine man," so that Jesus began to be understood as a "divine man."

No claim is made that the above brief summary proves, or even attempts to give evidence for, the correctness of this explanation for the development of one element of the Gospel tradition. That requires much more space than is available here and has already been repeatedly done in the studies of the Gospels of the past two generations, a selection of which is included in the bibliography appended to this chapter. Skeptical readers are urged to pursue the matter for themselves in the secondary literature and in their own detailed investigations of the Gospel texts, which of course contain the

Diagram 4

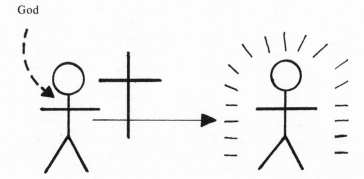

God

A.D. 30
Jesus' miracles
manifest God's presence.

A.D. 50
Tradition isolates and
enhances miracles, under-
cutting Jesus' humanity.

only evidence we have for any hypothesis about the nature of the Gospels, including the most traditional hypotheses.

Here I wish only to point out that the increasing emphasis on miracles in the Gospel tradition, culminating in the telling of stories about Jesus in which he appeared, or seemed to appear, as a "divine man," was by no means done by the early church with the intent of falsifying the A.D. 30 event of Jesus. In telling stories of Jesus in the 30-70 period, the church was concerned neither to fictionalize the Jesus-story nor be historically accurate concerning it; the church's concern was rather to interpret the saving significance of the Jesus-event. As Edward Lohse has written, "No statement which the early church transmitted about the earthly Jesus was intended to speak merely of a past event. But all that was told of Jesus' deeds and words was intended to proclaim the living Christ."[3] The church used whatever forms were available to proclaim its faith that in Jesus, the man of Nazareth, God had acted for the salvation of humanity. In its effort to communicate this faith to people to whom the Scriptural categories "covenant," "promise," and "Christ" were vague or meaningless, new categories that were familiar to the culture were pressed into service, usually in a process that was intuitively correct, though largely unself-conscious.

"Christ," for example, was a traditional Jewish term for the ultimate bringer of salvation whom God would send at the climax of history to redeem his creation and save his people. To say "Jesus is the Christ" was meaningful where the Jewish expectation of "the Christ" was part of the culture. Whether it was accepted or rejected, "Jesus is the Christ" was a meaningful statement. But how was the church to preach that "the Christ" had come in the Gentile world where a "Christ" was not expected?[4] Other categories which *were* meaningful were adopted and adapted as a way of communicating the ultimate significance of Jesus. "Divine man" was one such category which some Christians used to interpret the significance of the saving act of God in the Jesus-event. In this category, the life of Jesus appeared as an epiphany of the power of God. Since this is a crucial point, and since Mark includes so much of this kind of material, it needs to be amply illustrated.

Epiphany Christology in the Miracle Stories

"Epiphany" means "manifestation," or "revelation," a "making-obvious." In the Hellenistic world, "epiphany" was a word commonly used for the manifestation of the power of a god. Thus the Hellenistic king Antiochus Epiphanes, for example, was so called because he claimed, as did many oriental rulers, to be not a mere human being but a manifestation of the deity. "Epiphany Christology" is thus a term used to describe that kind of thinking about Jesus which interpreted his ministry as a manifestation of the power of God. During the period of oral tradition between Jesus and the Gospels, each miracle story was an expression of epiphany Christology, in that the miracle stories tended to present the earthly life of Jesus as a manifestation of God's power. In this Christology, the basic Christian affirmation that God has acted in Christ for our salvation was pictured in such a way that each miracle story became a "gospel in miniature" which portrayed the saving event as a whole.

What does it mean to describe the Jesus-event as the "saving-event"? Language about "being saved" may conjure up emotional, revivalistic, keep-my-soul-from-going-to-hell pictures which are no longer meaningful to us. But we are not the first generation to need "salvation" terminology to be pictured for us in some other way before it has much meaning. The problem was also faced in the first decades of the church's life, and the way it was dealt with then may be instructive for us.

Mark, and the pre-Markan tradition, identified "salvation" with "life." In Jesus' encounter with the rich young man in 10:17-31, for instance, the terms "be saved" (10:26), "enter the kingdom of God" (10:25), and "eternal life" (10:17) are all used to mean the same thing—the goal of all humanity's searching and striving, fulfillment of life. In such expressions, the adjective "eternal" is not simply a quantitative term when it modifies "life," to mean "live forever and ever," but is a *qualitative* modifier: life as it was meant to be, the life of the age to come when God has destroyed all the threats to genuine living, life that is "really living." Thus Mark can sometimes simply equate "enter the kingdom of God" with "enter life" (9:43, 45, 47). To receive salvation, to "be saved," is to receive the gift of life from God, to have all the threats to life overcome, to be saved from the enemies of life that rob it of being really life.

But this discussion is much more abstract than Mark and his tradition in fact make it. In the pre-Markan tradition, one way the church confessed its faith that in the Jesus-event God had acted for our salvation was to tell a story in which some deep human need was pictured, a story in which life (=salvation) was threatened or already lost. Into this situation strides Jesus, the mighty Son of God, who is not helpless in the face of human need. He acts, by his divine power, to deliver us from that which is robbing us of life. The situation of need and the deliverance are pictured in this-worldly terms, since they are portrayed as scenes from the earthly ministry of Jesus, but each story points beyond the particular situation of a few people in Galilee in A.D. 30 to the human situation generally, and to God's act in Jesus to deliver us from the tyranny of that situation. Although the stories deal with "ordinary" needs, it is humanity's ultimate salvation that is pictured, and ultimate deliverance to "eternal life" of the "kingdom of God" that is proclaimed. But this too is more discursive and abstract than the miracle stories make it. We do better simply to look at some of them with the preceding discussion in mind. In the following I interpret the miracle stories in a somewhat sermonic mode to correspond to this original form: They were *kerygma* (=preaching), not biography.

Deliverance from the Enemies of Life: Hunger
Mark 6:30-44; 8:1-10

These two stories of miraculous feedings were probably variations of the same story. Multitudes of hungry people are present. Hunger is the perennial human situation, as even we well-fed modern Western folk are

27

beginning to realize. Hunger keeps life from being what it should be. Hunger is a monster which, even when it does not succeed in literally destroying life physically (which has happened and is happening to more humans than most of us can imagine), perverts it into a subhuman scratching about for the next meal. It transforms human beings who were created to love and be loved into animals competing with each other for bare existence that is not life.

This obsession with getting something to eat, even at the expense of my neighbor or my father, has not been the personal experience to many who are reading this. But the picture burned into our memories by Elie Wiesel's stories from the Nazi concentration camps[5] exposes hunger as the demon who, even if I survive, delivers me into the hands of a pseudo-life that is a living death. Starving is not life; being hungry is not life; even surviving is not life. Life is sitting down with one's fellows in the presence of plenty, giving thanks for it, and sharing it. Thus the Jewish tradition sometimes pictured the ultimate salvation of the world as the "Messianic Banquet" (e.g., Isaiah 25:6-8, Matthew 8:11, 1 Q Sa [a manuscript from the Dead Sea Scrolls]), a great feast at the end of history when all God's people sit down together around a great table at which there is food and fellowship for all—life.

Look again at the stories of the feedings of the 5,000 and of the 4,000. There is the situation of the hungry multitudes, the inability of themselves or the disciples to do anything about it, indeed the conviction that there is nothing that anyone can do about it. Hunger, competition, and dehumanization have the last word. It appears that this is the way life is, and one should try to get what one can for oneself. But in the Gospel story, this which seems to be the ultimate word about life, though real, turns out to be only the penultimate word. Jesus gives the people food, gives them life, and they sit down and give thanks and celebrate together the good gifts of life. Thus the story has taken on, in the process of being handed on in tradition, some of the features of the "Messianic Banquet," and of the church's celebration of the Eucharist. For the Eucharist, too, like this story, is also a testimony to, and anticipation of, the ultimate salvation to which God's people look forward and in which they already participate on the basis of God's saving act in Christ.

I am suggesting that the reason this story was told in the early church was not simply to report a curious thing that happened on a Galilean hillside. It was told in order to picture the saving event which the church believed had taken place in Jesus. There the human situation is pictured. There Jesus is pictured as God's act to deliver us from that damnable situation. I am not suggesting that allegorization of the miracle stories is the proper way to interpret them. They are not allegories. In an allegory, each item in the story is a code or symbol for some other reality. We see an example of allegorical interpretation in Mark 4:14-20, which explains the meaning of each item in the parable of the sower. If the story of the feeding of the 5,000 were interpreted as an allegory, each item in the story would have some particular meaning: the five loaves representing the five books of Law, or the five cardinal virtues; the two fish representing the two tables of the Law or the two sacraments, etc. The miracle stories in the Gospels are not allegories, but neither are they simply reports. They are symbolic stories, narrative symbols, which were told not because they point back to some interesting event in the life of Jesus but because they point beyond themselves to the ultimate salvation of humanity, and to the act of God in Jesus which gives ultimate deliverance.

Such a story declares that even if hunger "gets me," devastates me—physically, or, perhaps worse, by letting my physical life continue but only as a distortion of human life—still, hunger has not destroyed me. Hunger does not have the last word. God-in-Christ has the last word and is able to save even when there is no earthly reason for any longer believing in salvation.

This miracle story, like every New Testament miracle story about Jesus, is a testimony that God has acted in Christ for our salvation. Whoever believes *that* believes what the early church proclaimed when it told this story about Jesus, whatever he may believe happened or did not happen on the Galilean hillside. Whoever denies *that* denies the gospel which is enshrined in the story, however much he may believe in the multiplication of loaves and fishes on a certain day in A.D. 30. Most of those who told this story in the early church probably did believe they were relating an actual event in Jesus' ministry. But this was not the reason the story was preserved and told. The intent was to portray the meaning of the *whole* Jesus-event,[6] to present in a picture the significance of what God had done for the world in Jesus.

The *intent* of the story was to preach the gospel, not to make pronouncements about what kind of *being* Jesus of Nazareth was. But the inevitable *result* of this mode of preaching the gospel was to suggest that Jesus does not share our human weaknesses but is a "divine man." His life is not a human life but an epiphany of the divine power.

Deliverance from the Enemies of Life: Nature
Mark 4:35-41

The disciples, some of whom are experienced sailors, are in their boat in the middle of the lake. By chance, a storm comes up. It could not have been predicted, and there is nothing anyone can do about it. In spite of their skill and their best efforts, their boat is sinking. They are about to be done in by blind nature, a neutral machine-like cosmos which knows nothing of the human lives it grinds up in its cogs. What a stupid, meaningless way for a human life to end! Everyone who has had a near-miss on the highway or runway knows the feeling, the angry and helpless *human* feeling of almost having the only life one has snuffed out by blind, unfeeling nature. Though death is always the enemy, some deaths at least have a modicum of dignity and meaning: the crown of a long and full life or a sacrifice for some noble cause or other. But to have the whole enterprise of living canceled without warning by some chance combination of atmospheric conditions over a small lake in Galilee? Each of us could join in the angry cry, if there were anyone to hear: "Don't you *care* that we are dying?" (4:38).

Again, this is not allegorizing the story into the "storms of life" and how Jesus can calm them. Rather, the point is that the fragile human situation is pictured, our about-to-be-lostness which gnaws away in the subterranean rooms of our consciousness even on our best days. Again: Is this the last word about human life? That it can end suddenly and absurdly, so we should "get all the gusto" we can while we are here? Is the only laughter in this world gallows humor? Is the only song whistling in the dark?

In this story, though the disciples are at the mercy of blind chance, Jesus is master. He commands the storm to stop, and the disciples are given their lives back. Here is a picture of salvation, a picture that points beyond an incident on a Galilean lake to the ultimate problem of humanity and its ultimate solution.

The story does not promise that Jesus will appear and get us out of any trouble. The Markan church, which had seen Christians burned as flares in Nero's gardens, knew better than that. But the believer in what this story has to say knows that, when he is up against the storm, he is in the care of One who is nature's Creator and Master and who will not let his life finally be the victim of the storm, even when he must go down with his ship. The story does not just relate an incident from within the life of Jesus; it expresses the faith of the church in the salvation wrought by God in the whole Christ-event. But: In the story, though *we* are weak, Jesus is not like us. He is an epiphany of the power of God. Although the story functions to tell us something about the meaning of salvation, it has a Christological by-product: a picture of Jesus as a superhuman Son of God.

Deliverance from the Enemies of Life: The Demonic
Mark 5:1-20

Already in the story of the stilling of the storm, we have met something of the demonic in this world. For *us,* a storm is impersonal and mechanical, a matter of temperature, humidity, barometric pressure, and wind velocity. But in 4:39, Jesus rebukes and commands the storm with the same words he had used in exorcising a demon in 1:25. There is something devilish about the world itself; when a fragile human life is up against it, the cosmos takes on a demonic aspect.

Of course, I am not suggesting that the molecules of the material world are somehow inhabited by impish evil beings who bend them to our destruction. I only intend that we recognize, in the picture of Jesus rebuking the demon-storm, something of our own feeling when we sense that we are in the grip of something beyond our power to deal with, something awesome and destructive, an *evil* something. To us the very impersonality of the storm is its demonic aspect. We know that there is no use pleading with the flood, that there is no bargaining with the storm, that no rituals affect the path of the tornado. We are not only helpless before that, we are anxious and angry, precisely because "there is nothing we can do about it."

In the many exorcism stories in the synoptic Gospels, this demonic factor in our human situation is made individual and personal. In the "boundary-situations" of life, we know that not only nature but those about us and sometimes we ourselves are in the grip of something over which we have no control, that we are in danger of losing our grip on ourselves. Not only does this come home to us when mental illness strikes someone close to us, but even when we are most clearheadedly capable of thinking through our real situation, it may dawn upon us that the battle is already lost, that we have already been taken over by something bigger than we are, an evil something. Whether it be conceptualized as the combination of chromosomes in our genetic history which has made us what we are, or as long-forgotten events in our babyhood which still cast their spell over us in our subconscious, or as the political-economic system in which our lives are already enmeshed before we ever become conscious of making any decisions about it, or whatever: we know that *we* are not in control of our lives, that we can't simply decide what to do and be, and then pull it off. I am not who I "really" am—God! I don't even know what that would be—but I know that my name is Legion, that I am a multitude of things that I have been made into by powers over which I have no control. Is that the last word about my destiny, always to be possessed, never to possess?

In the story in Mark 5:1-20, there are elements of ancient views about demons, mythology about their cure, and folk-humor about an unbelievably large herd of hogs. There is also the conviction that because of what God has done in Jesus, there is salvation even from the demonic that infects our own persons. There is one who can let us sit down, clothed in our right mind, and be ourselves. The early church believed this not because they had developed certain theories about human personality or ultimate reality but because of something that had happened in the life, death, and resurrection of Jesus. Although it is probably the case that Jesus did function as an exorcist during his ministry (as some other Jewish rabbis did), this story was told not to memorialize an incident at Gerasa (or Gergasa, or Gadara; the traditions and manuscripts locate the story at different places) but to declare the meaning of the whole Christ-event: God is victor over the demonic. But again, note that this results in picturing Jesus not as weak-like-us but as strong-not-like-us.

Deliverance from the Enemies of Life: Guilt
Mark 2:1-12

People bring to Jesus a man who cannot come himself. He is in need; he is paralyzed. But he does not know the nature of his need. He wants simply to walk about like others. But he is met with the authoritative-gracious word of Jesus, "My son, your sins are forgiven."

Here too, the human situation is pictured: guilt. Most of our conversation about guilt today is about guilt *feelings,* so that if we talk about guilt at all, it is to assure each other that we are OK and shouldn't feel guilty, or occasionally to chide each other for "laying guilt" on someone. If we feel guilty, we think we shouldn't. We assume that guilt feelings can be made to evaporate by heeding the exhortations not to feel guilty. But the man in the story didn't feel guilty. He *was* guilty. Like the rest of us, he was hopelessly bogged down in a morass of objective guilt that is more than a mere feeling. We eat while others starve; we become winners only by making someone else into a loser; we are guilty by our involvement in the human condition. And besides that, with malice aforethought we have done specific things that are evil. This is true whether or not we feel guilt.

Jesus pronounced forgiveness—unasked for, unearned, unpurchased. He did not first try to generate some guilt feelings which he could then assuage. He did not first try to crank up "conviction for his sins" in the poor man, a process the revivalistic tradition of American Christianity has refined into a science. The Jesus of this story assumes that to be human is to be guilty, just as does the Lord's Prayer. That is, the Jesus of this story already looks at the human scene from the divine perspective. He does not look at us with the level gaze of a *fellow* human being but from somewhere beyond us, from God's side. Already there is something of the transcendent, the miraculous, in this. But the actual pronouncement of forgiveness itself is certainly something that only God can do, as the scribes recognized (2:7). Although in its present form the story of forgiveness is encapsulated within another miracle story, that of the healing of the paralyzed man, the inner story too is that of a miracle. The word of forgiveness is a divine word, a word that we can never speak to ourselves, that we can never speak to each other on our own. As in the other miracle stories, the helpless human situation is pictured, the situation in which we are robbed of life by some overpowering enemy, in this case guilt, a situation from which Jesus delivers us by the power of God in him. In this case what is true in all the miracles is starkly clear: Jesus acts in the place of God (the scribes were right, 2:7). In these stories, if Jesus were only a man like ourselves, each story would, as to its literary genre, be a tragedy.

Deliverance from the Enemies of Life: Loneliness
Mark 6:45-50

Again the disciples are in their boat in the middle of the sea, but this time they are alone. They do what they are supposed to do, "making headway painfully," but they are in the boat and Jesus is on the land. He who made God real to them, who himself mediated the presence of God, was not with them, and *could* not be with them, for they were in the middle of the sea, and he was on the land with no boat. It was a time of the absence of God, of knowing that one is, after all, an orphan in the universe, that whether it be lamented or celebrated, *we* are the highest that there is in the universe, the leading edge of an evolution that is itself mindless, though it has now generated minds that can know they are alone. Hermann Hesse speaks for all of us who have ever scratched the surface of the human situation:

Seltsam, im Nebel zu wandern!
Einsam ist jeder Busch und Stein,
Kein Baum sieht den andern
Jeder ist allein.

Voll von Freuden war mir die Welt,
Als noch mein Leben licht war;
Nun, da der Nebel fällt,
Ist keiner mehr sichtbar,

Wahrlich, keiner ist weise,
Der nicht das Dunkel kennt,
Das unentrinnbar und leise
Von allen ihn trennt.

Seltsam, im Nebel zu wandern!
Leben ist Einsamsein.
Kein Mensch kennt den andern,
Jeder ist allein.[7]

My rough translation:

How strange, to walk in the fog!
Every bush and stone is alone.
No tree sees another.
Each is alone.

Once my world was full of friends,
When my life was still light;
Now, since the fog has fallen,
No one is visible.

Truly, no one is wise,
Who does not know the darkness
That inevitably and softly
Separates him from everyone.

How strange, to walk in the fog.
Life is lonesomeness.
No person really knows another.
Each one is alone.

We can cower together in the boat, be present to each other, try to overcome our cosmic loneliness with a local togetherness, or throw ourselves into the work with a "the-main-thing-is-to-get-this-damned-boat-across-the-lake" flair. What neither we nor any human comrade can do is to speak a word that comes from beyond, from the Mission Control of the universe, which says "Take heart, it is I; have no fear" (6:50). Whoever wonders if Jesus really was able to defy the law of gravity has missed the word which this story wants to say, as has the person who dogmatically declares that of course Jesus could walk on water when he wanted to. The form of this story is very much like the resurrection stories,[8] which already indicates that the Jesus-event is looked at as a whole, is looked *back* at, from this side of Easter. As in the Easter stories, it is the *resurrected* Christ who is present in this story: the Christ who can be present even when the doors are locked for fear (John 20:19), when his followers walk along a lonely road without hope, or when they break bread together (Luke 24:13-32). This story has little interest in relating to us a once-upon-a-time interesting thing that happened to the disciples in A.D. 30, but it does ask us whether we can believe that, because of what God has done in the Christ-event, we can never get into a situation in which God cannot be present to us. It was impossible that Jesus should come to them in the boat, but he came, and he comes to us, whatever metaphysical or moral bridges we may think we have burned behind us, however far back on the shore we may have left Jesus. The gospel is proclaimed in this story. But the by-product of portraying Jesus in this way is a picture of Jesus who walks on the water, who is like God, but not like us.

Deliverance from the Enemies of Life:
Meaninglessness and Aimlessness
Mark 1:16-20; 2:13-14

Four men in the fishing business are going about their daily work. A figure they have never seen before appears and speaks one brief sentence, "Follow me and I will make you become fishers of men." And they do it. A little later, Jesus speaks only two words to Levi the tax clerk: "Follow me." Without a question, objection, or explanation, he too begins to follow.

These too are miracle stories, as miraculous as anything in the Gospel. People are there, doing what people do, at their fishing or tax-collecting business. Blue and white collars, with their families and hired men, and without them, patriotic and not-so-patriotic. We recognize the cross-section of humanity, and know that some did what they did with a sense of purpose and meaning, some lived lives of quiet desperation behind their fishermen's or accountants' masks, and others had never given it a thought, never looked past the end of their fishing poles or desks. Here there is no "human problem," no "threatening situation" from which to be saved.

But the situation is parallel to that of the guilty paralytic who supposed that paralysis was his only problem, the one who didn't know guilt until he was faced with forgiveness. So also, meaninglessness is sometimes recognized only when it is placed beside meaning. Into these scenes at the lakeside and the tax office, steps Jesus with his call, "Follow me." Psychologizing will do no good here, nor will efforts to link these stories with other supposedly prior scenes in which Jesus has already met these disciples and prepared them for his call. To understand the story in Mark, we must take it as it is in itself, and it pictures a miracle. Without introduction, he knows them and knows that he wants them. By his mighty word, which works by its own power, Jesus calls people to a life of discipleship which gives them their reason for living, which fulfills their conscious-or-unconscious quest for meaning, the one thing which is worth leaving everything (1:18, 20; 2:14).

They follow entirely on the basis of his call. There is no examination of his credentials, no witnessing of his miracles (except the call itself), no comparing of his teaching with Confucius, Buddha, or the Maharishi. The hearer-reader of the story can give no explanation of *how* the call generates faith and following, any more than he can explain how Jesus comes to the disciples on the seas or calms the storm. He cannot explain how a world came into existence from nothing, a world which was also spoken into being by the creative word of God.

34

The word "call" is used of Jesus' act (1:20). This is the word repeatedly used in the early church for the act of God in creating the church (e.g., Romans 8:29-30; 9:11-12; 1 Corinthians 1:9; 7:17; Ephesians 4:1; 1 Peter 1:15, etc.). It speaks of the sovereignty of God, whose own mighty word goes forth and creates faith in response to it. No one can simply crank up faith within himself. The guideline that gives meaning to our life, the way out of the pit, is not spun out of ourselves, spiderlike, but is let down to us from somewhere. We do not figure out the meaning of our being here by looking within ourselves; nor is it something which we can say to each other. It can come only as a word from God. Again, this story does not merely speak of an A.D. 30 transaction between Jesus and some Galileans. It pictures the new dimension that has been created in the human situation by the act of God in the Christ-event as a whole. In these stories, too, Jesus is not one of us. He acts in the place of God.

Deliverance from the Enemies of Life: Sickness

Mark 1:29-34, 40-45; 2:1-12; 3:1-6, 7-12;
7:31-37; 8:22-26; 10:46-52

Sickness is the enemy of life. Just as salvation, *salus,* means health or wholeness, so sickness is the representative of death. "In the midst of life we are in death" is understood not just by the bereaved but by the sick. Those who wrote the psalms called "laments" for the hymnbook of ancient Israel understood this, and provided songs and prayers for the sick and those who had recovered from sickness. In these songs the existential truth comes to expression that to be in the grip of sickness is already to be in the hands of death. Death is not the enemy who only waits for life to be over to take us to the grave. It already reaches up out of the grave and places its slimy tentacles on us, keeping life from being *life,* though we go on breathing (Psalm 6; 22:14-15; 31:9-10; 41:1-10; 55:4-5; 56:13 [cf. v. 8]). These psalms emphasize the rupture in human *fellowship* that happens to the sick person too (cf. Mark 5:25 ff.).

When one gets sick, is life over? Is the fate of the blind, the deaf, the cripple, the leper, the diseased simply to remember what might have been, how he or she could have "really" lived "if only . . ."? Does the quasi-death which is sickness win? Does it succeed in robbing us of our life?

And we cannot heal. Thank God in some cases we can do things which expedite healing, promote healing, allow healing to take place. But seen from one point of view, healing is a mystery of the organism that works by itself; seen from another, it is the gift of God.

In the numerous healing stories about Jesus which circulated in the early church, several of which Mark included in his Gospel, the helpless, sick human situation is pictured; sometimes the hopelessness of any human help is emphasized (e.g. 5:26) and then Jesus steps into the situation, usually at his own initiative, and performs the healing act of God. It would be a mistake to understand the healing stories as allegories of the ultimate human situation, as though the persons in the stories were not sick people but only ciphers for sick humanity. But it would also be a mistake to hear the stories as mere reports of what the individual faith-healer Jesus once did for some sick Palestinians who were fortunate enough to be sick in his geographical and temporal vicinity. No, the early church preserved and retold these stories because they pointed beyond themselves. They somehow pictured the salvation-event as a whole, that salvation event which has been accomplished by God for humanity as a whole. According to the Christian gospel, God overcame the enemies of life by acting for us in Christ, an act which gives us life even if we are sick our whole life long.

In these stories, we could not imagine that Jesus *himself* was ever sick. He stands on the side of God and must be so pictured if he is to represent the answer to our human problem rather than another example of it.

Deliverance from the Enemies of Life: Death
Mark 5:21-43

No author of any New Testament book would recognize the contemporary talk of death as "natural" and "beautiful." Death is the enemy of life, the ultimate enemy (1 Corinthians 15:26). This is seen clearly in the death of a twelve-year-old. To impress this upon us with poignant clarity, Mark has taken two miracle stories and inserted one into the other. (This is a frequent Markan literary device which is more than "stylistic": besides 5:21-43, cf. 3:22-30; 6:14-29; 11:15-20; 13:5-27[?]; 14:1-11; 14:18-25[?]; 14:53-72).

A little girl lies dying. It is the death of hope, the death of joy. Her father, a religious man, a man of faith, believes that Jesus can heal her. Good news! He finds Jesus, who agrees to come. Shattered hope is reborn. If only they can get there in time! While there is life, there is hope.

They are stopped! No, worse than that. Jesus has stopped voluntarily for a sick woman. But there is no need to *stop,* actually—she has already been healed, just by the surreptitious touch of his garment as he went by. But why is there *delay* now, with my little girl looking down the road, wondering if we will get there in time? Anyway, this woman has put up with her malady for years and could come and be healed on any other day. Why this palaver? Jesus must get there before it is *too late.*

"Your daughter is dead. Why trouble the teacher any further?" Why indeed?

There is no way to express the tragedy of the death of a twelve-year-old girl. But what is already infinite is magnified in this case by the realization that it could have been prevented. If not by us, by God, if there is a God who hears the prayers of twelve-year-old dying girls. "Your daughter is dead; why trouble the teacher any further?" But whether said with anger or resignation, it is logical and reality-accepting. However, Jesus ignores it (5:36) and leads the way to the girl's house. Amidst the jeers of those mourners who can switch from wailing to heckling without effort, he pronounces those words which only God can pronounce at the Last Day: "Little girl, I say to you, arise." Even when it's too late, it's not too late.

We may now draw together, in summary form, the results of our study of the miracle-story way of confessing faith in Christ that was used in the early pre-Markan church.

36

(1) At one level, before the stories were placed together in the Gospel, each story should be seen as an individual picture, not as part of a series. This is the insight and value of form criticism. Each story was told in order to hold up a picture of the meaning of Jesus' life seen as a whole, not as a fragment of Jesus' biography. In the oral tradition stage, what each story had to say had to be said from within the story itself, not in relation to other aspects of Jesus' life or other traditions about him. From one point of view, the whole meaning of Jesus' life, death, and resurrection is summed up in the single story of releasing Jairus' daughter from death or the paralytic from guilt.

(2) The message of salvation by Christ is presented *by means of* a story in the A.D. 30 ministry of Jesus but is told from the perspective of the time after the cross and resurrection, looking back on the whole of the Christ-event and interpreting its significance. In each story, one of the deepest human needs is presented: food and fellowship at the table, deliverance from the chance and fate of blind nature, from the supra-human demonic structures in which our lives are enmeshed, from guilt, from loneliness, meaninglessness, sickness, and the ultimate enemy who is also present in all the preceding—death. The miracle story declares that God has responded to these needs, has acted in Christ to deliver us from those powers that pervert our lives and threaten to destroy them. Though each story is set in the A.D. 30 ministry of Jesus in Galilee and Judea, it is not fundamentally a story of *Jesus* at all, but a testimony of what God has done through the one who is now the crucified and risen Lord. There is thus an important sense in which the story of Jairus' daughter is more concerned with the truth of the church's proclamation that God raised up Jesus than it is with a story about Jesus' raising a little girl, though these are related. It is a story which has more to do with Jesus' resurrection than a little girl's resuscitation. It asks us whether we believe that God raised up Jesus, rather than whether Jesus resuscitated a little girl. The question of God and the meaning of existence is raised by the death of little girls; the divine response to this question is found in the life-cross-resurrection event of Jesus. Our experience is that when little girls die, as they do, no one shows up to bring them back to life. But life in such a world is different if this is a world in which Jesus has lived, died, and been raised than if not.

(3) We should then be clear about what the miracle stories ask us to believe, what it means to "believe the Bible" at this point. If each story is fundamentally a testimony to the saving significance of the Christ-event, then the question of "what really happened" (in A.D. 30), "did Jesus walk on the water or not," etc., becomes a second-rank question. It is still a valid question, one that may be dismissed from neither the "miracle-believer" nor the "miracle-denier" side. But it is a question secondary to what the story wants to say to us. It is the kind of question that is to be settled by critical historical study, a study which is never divorced from the presuppositions of the historian, whether these be "believing" or "unbelieving" when it comes to miracles.

So those who investigate the matter (as opposed to those who, from either side, settle it in advance by their own dogma) will arrive at different results, that is, honest differences of opinion concerning which miracle stories in the New Testament, if any, report substantially what happened in the life of Jesus and which do not. For instance, many scholars who would accept the healing stories as substantially historical would question the historicity of Jesus' withering the fig tree with a curse (Mark 11:12-14, 20) or paying his taxes with money miraculously obtained from a fish's mouth (Matthew 17:24-27).

But the stories do not ask us to believe some information concerning what actually happened in some incident in the life of Jesus, and indeed, they frequently give varying descriptions of the same event. (Compare, for instance, the account of raising Jairus' daughter in Mark 5:21-43 and Matthew 9:18-26, or the healing of the blind man [men] in Mark 10:46-52 and Matthew 20:29-34.) Thus, those who answer the question of "what really happened" in various ways, including diametrically opposite ways, may leave the question somewhat open. Neither need simply dismiss the other, for they are disagreeing about something that is not really the issue anyway. Believing something about "what really happened" in some purported incident in the A.D. 30 ministry of Jesus is not yet believing what these stories ask us to believe—that God has acted in Christ for our salvation.

Questioning or denying that a particular miracle story actually represents "what really happened" in A.D. 30 is not necessarily the same as questioning or denying that God has acted in Christ for our salvation. "Miracle believers" may learn that they are not yet included among believers in the Christian faith simply by virtue of their belief in miracles (although, of course, these are not *alternatives*), and "miracle-deniers" may learn that they have not thereby said no to the faith. The real question put to us by the miracle stories is "what really happened" *in the Christ-event as a whole,* whether this be thought of as filled with miracles (as some New Testament documents picture it) or not (as pictured by other New Testament writings).

The story of the raising of Jairus' daughter, for instance, as it was preached in the early church, claims that because of the God who is for us and with us, and who has made this known and put it into action by his saving act in the life, death, and resurrection of Jesus, we can never come into a situation of "being lost" because it is "too late" for us to really live. The good news, made known in Jesus' cross and resurrection, is not that if we are good the worst won't happen but that when the worst has happened, the possibility of life, real life, salvation, is there. The message of this story (bound up with *Jesus'* resurrection, not the little girl's resuscitation), declares that *no matter what* has already happened to us or in us, the gift of life is still offered to us by the God who creates out of nothing, justifies the ungodly, and raises the dead, who offers hope precisely when there is no hope (Romans 4:1-25). If the message of this story is true, no one need spend his days in nonlife, dreaming of what might have been "if only . . ." X hadn't already happened and destroyed life forever. No dead past may rob us of the present and the future. This is the good news witnessed to by the early church which told the miracle story, and whoever believes *this* has been grasped by the true miracle to which the story testifies, whether or not he regards the story itself as "factual."

(4) There are thus fundamental differences between the miracle stories about Jesus in the New Testament and the miracle stories of the Hellenistic "divine men." To begin with, for the "divine men" the miracle story itself was the focus of interest, belief, or nonbelief. It did not point to anything beyond itself. No one ever proclaimed that in Apollonius or Socrates God had acted for the salvation of the world. No one believed that the person of Apollonius had been exalted to the right hand of God, made the Lord of the Universe, or that he in his earthly life represented the disclosure of the ultimate Being of the universe. No one thought that he was the "eschatological" (=ultimate) figure, that his life was the eschatological event in history which gave meaning to all the rest. In sum: None of the miracle stories about any of the "divine men" proclaimed them as the Christ. The miracles of the "divine man" were ends in themselves, not signs pointing to something else. One heard the story, was perhaps entertained by it, believed it or didn't believe it, and passed on to other things, much as in a discussion of the existence of flying saucers in our own time. But one was not challenged to decide something about the whole meaning of the world and one's own life by the stories.

Unfortunately, many individuals in the church, past and present, have understood the miracle stories about Jesus as though they were no more than this, and have either made Jesus into another Hellenistic "divine man" (if one affirmed the historicity of the stories) or rejected the whole Jesus-story because it was so understood (if one denied the historicity of the stories). Both have made the unintentional, unconscious mistake of trying to interpret the New Testament stories as though they were simply "divine man" stories.

A second difference between the miracle stories concerning Jesus and those of the "divine men" is that the New Testament stories do not intend to affirm anything about the metaphysical nature of Jesus, about his "person." That is, they are not oriented to showing that he is "divine" and not "human." Apollonius' miraculous disappearance from Domitian's court was to prove that he was "not a mortal man," which is indeed the point of the whole collection of stories about him. But in the stories about Jesus, the issue is not Jesus' "divine nature" but the act of God in the whole Jesus-event.

In this whole discussion, we should keep in mind that in the first century there was a way available of telling miracle stories about Jesus which did not portray him as a divine being but as a thoroughly human person through whom *God* worked amazing deeds. This is the typical perspective on miracles of the Old Testament, which knows of only one God, but a God whose power is sometimes made available through a man such as Moses or Elijah. Miracle stories were told of both Moses and Elijah, but those Jewish monotheists who told them never for a moment supposed that this meant that Moses or Elijah were "divine" beings. In a Jewish environment where Old Testament models of thought were dominant, this was also the prevailing way in which the amazing healings and exorcisms characteristic of Jesus' ministry were understood. We can still observe this early understanding of Jesus' miracles in the "Q" materials, where Jesus' mighty deeds are understood as signs of the breaking in of the kingdom of *God*. But just as in Hellenistic Judaism Moses had already taken on "divine man" characteristics, so also when the stories about Jesus' mighty deeds began to be told in a Hellenistic environment where traditional Old Testament models of thought were not prevalent, the seductive possibility of understanding Jesus in "divine man" terms emerged.

The New Testament miracle stories differ from the Hellenistic tales of the divine men in a third important respect. Consider these words from Homer's *Odyssey*, XVII, 458ff:

> For holy gods, in the form of wandering foreigners, taking on various forms, often go through countries and cities, that they may see mortals' foolish misdeeds as well as piety.

This idea of the incognito deity who is still in full possession of his divine powers was common in New Testament times, as Acts 14:11-13 and 28:3-6 illustrate. There is a kind of *aloofness* from the human situation manifest in such statements, a kind of divine "slumming." The Jesus of the miracle stories is like the "divine men" in that he has the divine power, but the distant, nonbelonging note is rarely struck (a touch of it is in Mark 9:19, 23, perhaps, and it is more prevalent in the Johannine picture of Jesus). But the typical picture of Jesus in the miracle stories is that of one who, though his power transcends that of the human situation, is still involved in it, moved by it, and in fact has *more* compassion for it than the "ordinary" human beings in it (Mark 1:41; 3:1-6; 6:34; 8:2; 10:13-16, 46-52).

(5) If the adoption of the miracle story as a means of preaching the gospel is fraught with so much possibility of misunderstanding, we may ask why the early church adopted this method at all. And we should first note that not everyone in the early church did. Paul and the authors of the other epistolary literature rejected this genre of Christian witness. Paul, at least, did so intentionally, as we shall see, because he saw no way of overcoming its dangers. And the preceding discussion of several pages of more-or-less abstract, discursive reflection has seemed necessary for us to get the "message" of the miracle stories without being misled by surface misinterpretations. So why didn't the early church do the same, giving us abstract discussions of the meaning of the Christ-event and avoiding the possibilities of misunderstanding inherent in the inclusion of the stories themselves?

First, there was the point of contact in Jesus' life, the amazing phenomena which occurred in his presence, generating miracle stories which were continued in the church after Easter. There was a historical reason for miracle stories in the church, the historical facticity that went back into the A.D. 30 ministry of Jesus and which was not to be denied.

Second, there was the need to translate the Jewish images of "the Christ." Such images usually did not contain miracles; the typical Jewish expectation of "the Christ" was one of a royal military figure, not a miracle worker. When the church carried the gospel beyond Jewish frontiers, it used more understandable terms for purposes of communication. The "divine men" category was adopted and adapted.

But the main reason for the miracle stories was probably neither of these but rather the fact that there is no substitute for a story. The Christian gospel, expressed abstractly in the declaration "God has acted in Jesus for our salvation," can be expressed either by telling stories from Jesus' life or by telling what God did through him by "sending him into the world" and "raising him from the dead to sit at his right hand." The early church and the New Testament utilized both ways, as we shall see. The second way locates the transcendent element, the act-of-God-in-Jesus element, at the extremities of his earthly life: before Bethlehem and after Golgotha. This is the realm of myth, and talk of Jesus in mythical language was one of the primary means of interpreting the saving significance of the act of God in him. The church could have attempted to get by, as Paul did, without telling miracle stories about Jesus, but this meant that his transcendent, divine significance had to be expressed in creedal and mythical language. This has its own validity, as we shall see, but it has lost contact with the earthly life of Jesus and has no place for the stories of what he said and did as he walked and talked with his disciples in Galilee.

And the early church was not willing to limit its talk of Jesus to what could be said only by projecting his significance onto a cosmic, pre-existence or post-resurrection screen. An important part of the saving Good News was that Jesus had in fact lived in this world among human beings as a human being. So not only were songs sung and creeds recited that celebrated the pre-existent divine being who had come to earth and been raised back to heaven (Philippians 2:5-11; Colossians 1:15-20, etc.), but incidents were recounted that have their setting in the dusty villages of Galilee. As a complement to the mythical, creedal, propositional, discursive language preferred in the epistles, language which corresponds to the *life* of Jesus had to be anecdotal and pictorial. Story language which "gives us the picture" can be supplemented by, but never replaced by, discursive language. Remember, we are still talking about the early oral period, in which the elements of the Christian tradition were not yet put together into collected wholes but each individual story, creed, or song was circulated separately. In these oral stories, if it was to be shown that it was *God* who was active in the Jesus-event, then Jesus had to appear not as another weak human being like ourselves but as one full of the divine power.

All of this means that the above discussion, even if it should be found helpful for appropriating the message of the miracle stories, can never be taken as a substitute for reading the stories themselves. They are irreplaceable.

(6) So Mark does not attempt to replace the miracle stories in his tradition with something else, although, as we shall see, he was suspicious of the miracle-story *taken by itself* as an adequate means of affirming the Christian faith. But Mark did find a way to overcome the dangers inherent in miracle stories, and this enabled him to take over from his tradition a great mass of material which presented Jesus as a miracle worker and tended to represent him as a "divine man."

41

It is important to understand that Mark's suspicion of the miracle-story genre and its associated picture of Jesus as "divine man" was not expressed by "watering down" or softening the "divinity" of Jesus as it appears in these stories. Not only does Mark allow the "divine man" stories which came to him in his tradition to stand, some of which embarrassed later authors (7:32-35; 8:22-26, omitted by both Matthew and Luke, who otherwise adopt almost all of Mark's miracle stories); he intentionally extends and intensifies the claim to Jesus' divinity implicit in these stories in material edited by or composed by him.

A key example is 8:17-21. This is a scene almost certainly composed by Mark himself, since it comments on the meaning of both feeding stories, and since this combination was probably made by Mark himself. In this conversation with the disciples, Mark lets Jesus affirm the meaning of his ministry as it is portrayed in the miracle stories and Mark blames the disciples for not seeing this.

Another example is 14:61-62, also composed by Mark himself, in which Mark has Jesus say, for the first time in the Gospel, that he is the Christ, the Son of God, the Son of Man who is seated at the right hand of God, the eschatological Judge who will come at the end of time and exercise God's judgment. The one who here speaks declares himself to belong to the divine world, the same claim made by the miracle stories, and it is Mark himself who has placed this claim on Jesus' lips. Mark not only affirms the picture of Jesus as divine in the miracle stories; he does it ungrudgingly. He emphasizes it.[9]

(7) Finally, we must make clear the price that was paid by the early church by expressing its faith in God's act in Jesus in "divine man" terms. The Jesus who operates in these stories is no longer one of us. His life is an epiphany of the divine power. He is not human as we are human but, like the "divine man," is a heavenly visitor. However much he may be in the world, he is not of the world. The miracle stories contain no references to Jesus' humanity; in particular, references to suffering and dying are absent from them. They move in a different world from the world of crosses and crucifixions. The "divine man" Jesus does what only God can do. We have seen the value and importance of this.

To use the story of the raising of Jairus' daughter again as an illustration of something present in all miracle stories, we note that the only hope for the people in the story is for an act of God. This is good biblical faith, which does *not* believe in immortality, that is, that within human beings there is something inherently immortal, which cannot die. Biblical faith always presents hope for life beyond death in terms not of something that is true about human beings (that they are immortal) but in terms of something that is true about God (he raises the dead). So if there is any hope for the girl and her parents, that hope is exclusively in an act of God on their behalf. This is also the case with the problem of guilt: it takes an act of God to save us from it. And so with the other stories of human need, Jesus provides the answer. He does what is humanly impossible. Nothing is impossible for such a one. "With men it is impossible, but not with God; for all things are possible with God" (Mark 10:27).

The Problem with a "Divine Man" Jesus

All the preceding discussion has been necessary in order to understand the scene Mark portrays at the cross, when the chief priests hurl their mocking challenge: "Let the Christ, the King of Israel, come down now from the cross, that we may see and believe" (15:32). What happens when the "divine man" way of picturing the salvation event is extended to the crucifixion scene? The logical choices would seem to be clear-cut: (1) He wanted to come down, but couldn't (since he was *not* the divine Son of God he claimed to be—the logic of the high priests) or (2) He could have come down but didn't want to (since he *was* the divine Son of God he claimed to be—the logic of many traditional Christians).

Here, in this one darkly drawn scene, is presented the problem of believing in God while living in a world of evil. It is the problem of anyone whose eyes are opened to the crosses of this world, and who professes to believe in a God who is both supremely good and supremely powerful. Epicurus' ancient statement of the problem has both plagued believers (Augustine!) and encouraged unbelievers (Hume!) to remain so:

> Is he willing to prevent evil, but not able?
> Then he is impotent.
> Is he able, but not willing? Then he is malevolent.
> Is he both able and willing? Whence then is evil?[10]

The logic seems to present us with a clear either/or, from which there is no escape. Let us look more closely at each option in its Markan frame of reference. (Mark, who has composed this scene, is not untouched by the problem.)

The understanding of the chief priests, that Jesus was not the divine Son of God he claimed to be, is clearly a misunderstanding, or rather, a culpably false understanding. Mark's own faith, confessed from the first line of the Gospel onwards, constantly portrayed in the miracle stories, and explicitly reaffirmed at key junctures in the narrative throughout, is that Jesus is truly the divine Son of God (1:1; 1:11; 3:11; 5:7; 9:7; 13:32; 14:62; 15:39). The traditional understanding has often been that Mark operated with the same logic as the chief priests. It has been supposed that both Mark and his opponents, as represented by the chief priests, assumed that if Jesus were the Son of God, he of course could do what a divine being could do, namely call off the curcifixion by coming down from the cross. In this view, the difference between Mark and his opponents is solely that Mark affirmed Jesus to be such a Son of God, and the chief priests denied it, but both Mark and his opponents are assumed to *think* about the matter in the same *way,* to operate with the same logic.

Thus many forms of the Christian faith have supposed, with a certain inevitable logic, that if the Christian confession is true, that Jesus is the Christ, the Son of God, then what must be affirmed about this scene is that Jesus could have come down from the cross, but did not want to do so. How could it be supposed that Jesus was able to come down, but unwilling to do so? A certain theory of the atoning death of Jesus has been pushed in

43

here—something which Mark does not do. It is a theory which, taken with any degree of literalness at all, has its own problems, but one factor in its popularity in many streams of Christian tradition seems to be that it helps with the central problem of the mighty Son of God who nevertheless "suffered and died" on the cross. Those who hold this position seem driven by inexorable logic to affirm that Jesus could have come down but did not want to do so. Why? Because he had come into this world to give his life as a "ransom for many" (10:45). So he stayed on the cross, though he *could* have come down, in order to die for the sins of humanity. This is the conventional logic. But can such playacting be called "dying"?

Although Mark says much about Jesus' suffering and death, this one reference (10:45) and possibly 14:24 are the only places where Mark even approaches interpreting Jesus' death as a substitutionary atonement. Mark never relates Jesus' death to the removal of human sins, never makes the cross the ground of God's forgiveness. Of course, I am not denying that other New Testament writers do use the picture of the sin-offering as a means of interpreting the significance of Jesus' death (e.g., Matthew 26:28; Romans 5:6-11; 1 Corinthians 15:3; 2 Corinthians 5:14-21; Hebrews 9:11-26; 1 John 1:7; Revelation 1:5), that elsewhere Jesus' giving his life is related directly to our being forgiven by God.

Properly understood, this interpretation is a helpful and valid way of appropriating the meaning of Jesus' death. Here I am only concerned with pointing out that the exegetical basis for the idea of a substitutionary atonement as the meaning of Jesus' death *in Mark* is exceedingly slim, and that we should be wary of importing an idea apparently not of primary importance to Mark to explain a hard problem which Mark, with full awareness of what he is doing, presents to us. The idea that the Markan Jesus remained on the cross because he *wanted* to, rather than because he *had* to, seems to have been read not out of the text, but into it, because the logic seemed to demand it. The only alternative seemed to be the mocking unbelief of the chief priests.

But since this approach to understanding Jesus' death has been so common, we will look at it more closely and for the sake of the argument give its exegetical basis in Mark the benefit of the doubt. Thus this argument would say something like, "Christians in general in the early church believed that 'Christ died for our sins,' so Mark didn't have to *emphasize* this point. And 10:45 and 14:24 show that Mark wasn't opposed to this view. So, even if Mark didn't spell it out, he *must* have believed that Jesus *decided* to stay on the cross (to pay the penalty for our sins), since he certainly believed that Jesus was divine, and could have come down from the cross if he had wanted to, right?"

Not necessarily, but for the purpose of discussion, let us grant that Mark does understand Jesus' death to be "for our sins" in some sense necessary to facilitate God's forgiveness. Does the above argument represent what Mark wants to say about the death of Jesus? The fundamental objection to it, an objection which I think Mark would have been the first to raise, is that in such an explanation Jesus doesn't in fact "suffer and die" at all. A being who could come down from the cross is one who didn't have to go to the cross in the first place, who is only going through the motions of being crucified, who, if he feels anything, does so because, for whatever reasons, he decides to and allows himself to, knowing all along that whatever he "suffers" is at his own discretion. This is a "cool" Jesus, who is himself in control. The attempt to explain why Jesus endured the suffering of the cross by introducing a theory of the atonement when, as the "divine man" he didn't have to suffer, in fact makes Jesus' supposed suffering so different from the suffering and dying of the two men on either side of him as to disqualify such pretending from being suffering and death at all. In short, Jesus' suffering was not real but only a *seeming* to suffer; Jesus' humanity was not real, for he only seemed to be human.

This appears to be the logical consequence of accepting the "divinity" of Jesus. One stream of early Christianity did not hesitate to draw precisely this conclusion. They were called "Docetists" (from the Greek word *dokeo,* "seem"), "Seemists." In order to affirm and safeguard the true divinity of Jesus, they explained all the indications of Jesus' humanity in the tradition as instances where Jesus only seemed to be human. Books were written to express this understanding, and they had a wide circulation in the early church until they were excluded as heretical during the process of the formation of the canon. Some of these writings may appear grotesque to us, but they were done in the name of protecting the divinity of Jesus, and are but an extension of the same logic which we have been discussing above. Two examples will suffice:

1. The *Acts of John*[11]

The *Acts of John* was one of numerous "Gospels," "Acts," "Epistles," and "Revelations" excluded from the canon because it represented the Christian faith in an inadequate, perverted way. This book was probably written in the second century. The author intended only to glorify Jesus and the splendor of the Christian life but operated with a docetic understanding of Christ. In this document Jesus appears to John as an old man "having a head rather bald, but the beard thick and flowing," but at the same time to James as "a youth whose beard was newly come" (chap. 89). Sometimes he felt soft to the touch, other times "hard like unto stones," and sometimes could not be felt at all (chaps. 89, 93).

Once John pretended to be asleep and, in a *Twilight Zone*-like scene, beheld the supposedly physical body of Jesus conversing with its spiritual double lying beside it (chap. 92). John once "drew nigh unto him softly, as though he could not see me, and stood looking upon his hinder parts: and I saw that he was not in any wise clad with garments, but was seen of us naked, and not in any wise as a man" (chap. 90). This curious passage is reminiscent of Moses' being permitted to view only "the hind parts" of God (Exodus 33:23), and also probably intends to settle the question (negatively!) of whether the divine Jesus was equipped with human sexual and excretory features. Here as elsewhere in the *Acts of John,* Jesus is truly divine, but in no way human. Jesus complains to his spiritual double that his disciples do not sufficiently believe in him, "for *they* are men."

The author does not hesitate to carry through the logical consequences of this view of Jesus into the crucifixion scene.

I, then, when I saw him suffer, did not even abide by his suffering, but fled unto the Mount of Olives [to a cave] weeping at that which had befallen. And when he was crucified on the Friday, at the sixth hour of the day, darkness came upon all the earth. And my Lord standing in the midst of the cave and enlightening it, said: "John, unto the multitude below in Jerusalem I am being crucified and pierced with lances and reeds, and gall and vinegar is given me to drink. But unto thee I speak, and what I speak hear thou. I put it into thy mind to come up into this mountain, that thou mightest hear those things which it behoveth a disciple to learn from his teacher *and a man* [John] *from his God* [Jesus]" (chap. 97).

Here the divine Son of God *does* come down from the cross. He only appears to be suffering and dying. He reveals a glorified cross of light to John, the true "spiritual" cross and explains:

But this is not the cross of wood which thou wilt see when thou goest down hence: neither am I he that is on the cross. . . . I was reckoned to be that which I am not, not being what I was unto many others: but they will call me [say of me] something else which is vile and not worthy of me. . . . Nothing, therefore, of the things which they will say of me have I suffered (chaps. 99-101).

The "something" that is "vile and not worthy of" Jesus which will be said about him by less-enlightened Christians (in the author's view) is that Jesus truly suffered and died as a human being on the cross. But the author of the *Acts of John* knows that if Jesus were truly the Son of God, he could not have been impaled on the cross as a weak human being, but could have come down, and in fact did so. This author operates within the same logic as the chief priests in Mark's account of the crucifixion, affirms the premises which they deny, and extends this logic to its ultimate conclusion. John goes back to the crucifixion scene and laughs at the ignorance of those who suppose that Jesus really suffers (chap. 102).

2. *The Second Treatise of the Great Seth*[12]

This odd-sounding title belongs to a document of Gnostic Christianity found in the library of an ancient Gnostic-Christian sect in the Nile Valley at Nag Hammadi. In this manuscript from the third or fourth century (though composed earlier), Jesus is pictured as delivering an address to his followers after the resurrection. One quotation is sufficient to indicate the tenor of the whole:

I did not succumb to them as they had planned. But I was not afflicted at all. Those who were there punished me. And I did not die in reality, but in appearance, lest I be put to shame by them because these are my kinsfolk. I removed the shame from me and I did not become faint-hearted in the face of what happened to me at their hands. I was about to succumb to fear, and I [suffered] according to their sight and thought, in order that they may never find any word to speak about them. For my death which they think happened, [happened] to them in their error and blindness, since they nailed their man unto their death. For their Ennoias [mind, intent] did not see me, for they were deaf and blind. But in doing these things, they condemn themselves. Yes, they saw me; they punished me. It was another, their father, who drank the gall and vinegar; it was not I. They struck me with the reed; it was another, Simon, who bore the cross on his shoulder. It was another upon whom they placed the crown of thorns. But I was rejoicing in the height over all the wealth of the archons and the offspring of their error, of their empty glory. And I was laughing at their ignorance.[13]

Amidst the esoteric references to mysterious Gnostic teachings, the docetic Christology shines forth. Jesus caused Simon to be crucified in his place, caused Simon to appear to be Jesus, caused the soldiers and priests to think they were crucifying Jesus, who as the divine Son of God was all the while enjoying the spectacle from his box seat in the spiritual world, and laughing at the ignorance of these humans who supposed that he too was human. This view is not limited to one obscure document but, according to the second-century bishop Ireanaeus, was the official teaching of the sect of Basilides (*Against Heresies,* I, 24:4). Although told in a way that seems crass and grotesque to us, this viewpoint intended to be an affirmation of, and defense of, the true divinity of Jesus.

The *Acts of John* and *The Second Treatise of the Great Seth* are only two of a multitude of documents produced by early Christianity which the mainstream church branded as heretical and refused to accept as representing adequate Christian teaching. The word "heresy" may sound rather quaint to our ears, but it simply means "inadequate theology," theology which does not do justice to the faith it seeks to express. These documents, and many others like them, were considered heretical not because they did not consider Jesus divine, but because they did not consider him to be human.

We must not fail to notice the similarity between the three points of view of the chief priests in Mark's Gospel, the Docetists in the ancient church, and the brand of popular Christianity in our own day which we may designate "pop-Docetism." They are three variations of one position, sharing the same logic, the common denominator of which is "If he were truly divine, he *could* have come down from the cross." And that means he does not know what it is to share the weakness and victimization of a truly human life. Mark affirms, and wants us to affirm, that Jesus was "truly divine." But thus far the only way within this logical framework that we have been able to make this affirmation results in a perverted version of the Christian faith, in the paganization of the figure of Jesus into that of a Hellenistic "divine man" who can live among us but not with us, who can go through the charade of a crucifixion but not die with us. Within this logic, the only options seem to be unbelief or heresy.

This quandary should signal us that something is certainly amiss here, that we need to explore the whole question from a different starting point. What are the implications of choosing the other option to our original question: "If Jesus were truly *human,* he *could not* have come down from the cross"?

For Further Reading

Achtemeier, Paul J., "Gospel Miracle Tradition and the Divine Man," *Interpretation,* Volume XXVI, No. 2 (April 1972).

Bultmann, Rudolf, *The History of the Synoptic Tradition.* Harper & Row, 1963.

Cartlidge, David R., and Dungan, David L., *Documents for the Study of the Gospels.* Fortress Press, 1980.

Fuller, Reginald, *Interpreting the Miracles.* SCM, 1963.

Hadas, Moses, and Smith, Morton, eds., *Heroes and Gods: Spiritual Biographies in Antiquity.* Routledge and Kegan Paul, 1965.

Holladay, Carl, *Theios Aner in Hellenistic Judaism.* Scholars Press, 1977.

Kee, Howard Clark, *Miracle in the Early Christian World.* Yale University Press, 1983.

Richardson, Alan, *The Miracle Stories of the Gospels.* SCM, 1941.

Theissen, Gerd, *The Miracle Stories of the Early Christian Tradition.* Fortress Press, 1983.

Tiede, David Lenz, *The Charismatic Figure as Miracle Worker.* Scholars Press, 1972.

2

The Gospel as the Weakness of Jesus

The Humanness of Jesus in Mark
Paul and the Early Christian Kenosis Christology
The Kenosis Christology of Hebrews
The Kenosis Christology of Revelation
Kenosis Christology in the Pre-Synoptic Tradition

The Humanness of Jesus in Mark

Alongside the picture of Jesus who operates with superhuman power, Mark portrays Jesus as one who fully shares human weakness. We need feel no hesitation in speaking of the weakness of Jesus. It is biblical language (2 Corinthians 13:4). By using the words "weak" and "weakness," I do not mean that, by human standards, Jesus was a weakling, physically or as a personality. Mark, like the other Gospels, tells us nothing at all of Jesus' physique, so we have no reason to picture him romantically as an athletic type. But we have every reason to think of him as having a forceful personality. Yet neither the one nor the other is intended by referring to the weakness of Jesus. I am writing about the weakness that is inherent in humanity as such, the finitude and inabilities that come with the fact of existing as a human being.

It is true that Mark does not clearly use the word "weakness" with reference to Jesus (although in 14:38 Mark probably has Jesus refer to

49

himself as well as the disciples). But other New Testament writers speak explicitly of Jesus' weakness (2 Corinthians 13:4; Hebrews 4:15; 5:2). The absence of the word in Mark is only incidental, for he repeatedly portrays Jesus as sharing our human limitations.

Mark 1:1

"Jesus" is a human name, common in first-century Judaism. Josephus, a Jewish historian whose life overlapped that of Jesus, mentions eighteen different persons named Jesus. The New Testament itself mentions an ancestor named Jesus (Luke 3:29; the Hebrew equivalent "Joshua" in some translations), as well as a Christian disciple with this name (Colossians 4:11).

Mark 1:9; 10:18

Our first glimpse of Jesus in the Gospel of Mark is of one who has come from Nazareth in Galilee to stand in the same line with sinful human beings who are waiting to be baptized by John "for the forgiveness of sins" (1:4). Although Matthew later felt constrained to augment this passage with an explanation which puts Jesus' baptism in a different category from that of other human beings (Matthew 3:13-17), and Luke declines to narrate the baptism at all, referring to it obliquely as in the past (Luke 3:21), Mark has no such hesitation.

With this we should compare Jesus' response to the rich young man who addressed him as "Good Teacher": "Why do you call me good? No one is good but God alone" (10:18). Goodness is something which humans possess only relatively and derivatively, and only God possesses absolutely and inherently. The Markan Jesus here specifically places God in one category and himself in another. As in 12:29, 32, so here there seems to be an emphasis on the *oneness* of God. Jesus here shows the Jewish horror of calling anything or anyone "divine" except the one Creator God of Israel's faith. Jesus is not "a God," "another God." Donald Baillie rightly argues that "a God" cannot be a Christian expression, that it is a category of one and cannot have a plural.[14] Again, Matthew is later bothered by this, and rewrites Jesus' response to soften the distinction (Matthew 19:17). This does not necessarily mean that Mark considered Jesus a sinner. It simply means that he had no concern to deny that Jesus was, and that he has no qualms about placing Jesus in the same category as the rest of us sinful human beings. The distinct impression is of a life that enters fully into the human situation.

Mark 1:11

The voice from heaven at Jesus' baptism not only says "You are my beloved Son" (=truly divine) but also declares "with you I am well pleased," words which scholars take to be from one of the Greek versions of Isaiah 42:1, where God addresses his "servant." In view of other instances of Mark's use of imagery from the "servant of the Lord" passages to apply to Jesus (8:31; 9:12; 9:31; 10:33-34; 10:45; 14:24; 14:60-61; 15:4-5), this interpretation is probably justified. Who is this "servant"?

As described in the four "servant songs" in the later sections of Isaiah (42:1-4; 49:1-6; 50:4-9; 52:13—53:12), the "servant of the Lord" is a thoroughly human figure, who operates without violence but whose strength is his very vulnerability and tenderness (42:2-3). He has no power of his own but is totally dependent upon God (42:1; 49:5; 49:7-9), the "man of sorrows" whose mission ends in being rejected, beaten, and brutally killed "like a lamb that is led to slaughter" (52:13—53:9). Yet even in his suffering and death, it is recognized that God was acting through him to take away sins and that after his death God has vindicated the mission which he carried out in weakness (53:10-12).

Mark 1:35; 6:41; 6:46; 14:32-42

Human beings pray to God in praise and gratitude but especially in acknowledgment that they cannot live out of their own resources, that they are dependent on God's power to sustain their lives. Neither gods nor angels pray. Especially in the Gethsemane scene portrayed in Mark 14, Jesus' human weakness is expressed. "Distressed" and "troubled" (v. 33, RSV; "horror and dismay came over him," NEB), weighted down with deathly sorrow (v. 34), desiring human companionship in his time of need (vs. 34, 37), Jesus fell to the ground and cried out to God in prayer (v. 35).

This is not posturing, posing for a painting in church parlors, but the barely controllable anxiety of one facing death and shuddering before it. He prayed, "If it is possible . . ." A god does not say "if," does not speak of "possibilities," but Jesus is here the victim of possibilities, not their master. He is at the mercy of what is possible. He does not, godlike, have it in his own control. He does not want to die (v. 36). And it is truly as a man, more truly human than any of us, that he concludes his prayer: "Yet not what I will, but what thou wilt" (v. 36). The disciples sleep while he prays, but Jesus' observation that "the spirit indeed is willing, but the flesh is weak" probably contains less condescension than has been supposed. He included himself.

Mark 2:16

Jesus eats. Divine beings do not need to eat. True to the logic of the "divine man," the *Acts of John* represents Jesus as not eating but miraculously multiplying his own portion of food for the disciples (chap. 93).

Mark 4:38

Jesus sleeps. (Contrast the *Acts of John* 89, where Jesus closes his eyes occasionally—he blinks—to keep up appearances.) But the Jesus pictured asleep in the boat, in the care of his friends and in the realm of their competence, is a Jesus who gets tired as we get tired, who is weary with a human weariness.

Mark 5:30; 6:38; 9:16, 21; 13:32

Not omniscient, Jesus asks questions in order to obtain information. Even as "the Son," his knowledge is limited in contrast to "the Father" (13:32)!

Mark 3:21; 14:44

Jesus, considered deranged by his family or close friends (the Greek expression is ambiguous), is subject to seizure and arrest. When the officers come to take him, there is nothing unusual about him by which he could be identified. Judas must point him out with a prearranged signal. So human he was!

Mark 8:12

Here Mark takes up a tradition which had represented the life of Jesus as entirely devoid of the divine power. In response to the challenge that Jesus produce a "sign" (that is, some miracle that would legitimate him as divinely authorized), Mark represents him as categorically declaring that no sign would be given to that generation. The variant forms of the saying contained in Matthew 12:39; 16:4; and Luke 11:29 announce that only the sign of Jonah will be given. Matthew understands this as referring to the resurrection. Luke apparently refers it to Jonah's preaching. In either case, Jonah worked no miracles; he only announced the impending act of God. This saying in all its forms, but particularly in Mark, represents the ministry of Jesus at the farthest extreme from a series of miracles.

Mark 3:6; 8:31; 9:31; 10:33-34; 12:8; chaps. 14-15

Jesus dies. This is the most human of all acts. The theme of the death of Jesus could be said to dominate Mark's Gospel. The allusion is probably already there in the heavenly voice at his baptism (see above). It is darkly suggested in Jesus' dinner-party comment that the time would come "when the bridegroom would be taken away from them" (2:20). It is already plotted by the Pharisees and Herodians in 3:6, and from 8:27 on becomes the dominant theme of the narrative. Since Martin Kähler in the last century, Mark has frequently been called "a Passion narrative with an extended introduction,"[15] and it is true that the account of Jesus' last days, his betrayal, arrest, trials, and crucifixion, is told with much more detail than any other part of the story.

But even the "introduction" is already permeated with reference to the Passion. Beginning with 8:31, Jesus' approaching death is the programmatic theme of his teaching. Especially the three parallel "Passion predictions" (8:31; 9:31; 10:33-34), which recur in this section of the narrative like "the solemn tolling of a minute bell"[16] point out the centrality of suffering and death in the Markan Jesus' own understanding of his mission.

When Jesus is the subject, the verbs referring to his suffering and death are in the passive voice: He will "*be delivered* into the hands of men" or to the chief priests (9:31; 10:33), he will "*be rejected* by the elders and the chief priests and the scribes" (8:31), and he will "*be killed*" (8:31). When the verbs are in the active voice, Jesus is never the subject but the object: "*They will* kill him" (9:31), "*will* condemn him to death, and deliver him to the Gentiles; and *they will* mock him, and spit upon him, and scourge him, and kill him" (10:33-34).

We should remind ourselves that the word "passion" in such expressions as "Jesus' Passion," the "Passion Play," and the "Passion story" does not refer, as we might suppose, to the intense feelings involved in the story of suffering and death. "Passion" here is related to the word "passive." The Passion story is not the story of what Jesus did but what was done to him. He is not active but passive. In Mark, from the moment when he is "delivered into the hands of men" in Gethsemane, Jesus is entirely passive (14:43ff.). He works no miracles to restore the slave wounded by one of his disciples (14:47—contrast Luke 22:51). He is betrayed, denied, questioned, tried, convicted, abused, and killed, but others are the actors. He is the victim, engulfed by the circumstances. *He does not die; he is killed.* (But this is true of every human life. Life does not just quit. It is always stopped.)

The victimization of Jesus is graphically portrayed by the use of the Old Testament quotation from Zechariah 13:7 in Mark 14:27, where Jesus is the shepherd struck down by God. Furthermore, the wording of the Old Testament text has been altered from "strike the shepherd" in Zechariah to "I [*God*] *will* strike the shepherd" in Mark, making it clear that Jesus, in an even more direct way than Job, that paradigm of human suffering, is about to be smitten by God himself.

In Mark, Jesus does not carry his own cross (contrast John 19:17). Mark may even picture Jesus being physically carried to the place of execution. (The basic meaning of the Greek word *phero* is "carry," as in our word "ferry," though it can also mean simply "bring.") Even if not physically carried, Jesus is passively *brought* to the cross and does not actively *go* to it.

On the cross, Jesus shows none of the calm disposition of his affairs, the sovereign concern with others which we find in Luke and John, but Mark contains only two of the "seven last words" compiled from all four Gospels. There is only the cry of abandonment, the Old Testament prayer (Psalm 22:1) prayed by many trapped human beings who felt deserted by God, and the final inarticulate scream (15:34-37). Even the prayer was garbled and misunderstood by the bystanders (15:35-36). Just as Mark felt free to identify Jesus with sinful human beings at the beginning of his ministry, without any compulsion to explain that he was, after all, *different,* so at the end of his life the Markan Jesus dies rather nonheroically, rather more quickly than most men, in fact, without any qualifying explanations from Mark (cf. 15:44-45). This is the death of a man, and we feel it could have been our own. It is the final picture of Jesus in the Gospel of Mark. There are no resurrection appearances. (The authentic text of Mark, preserved in the oldest manuscripts, ends at 16:8. Later scribes supplemented Mark by adding vs. 9-20, which are found in many editions of the English Bible.)

Thus the last reference to Jesus in Mark, the word from the "young man" to the seekers on Easter morning (16:6) is an almost exaggeratedly human characterization: "Jesus" (the human name of a particular Jew, shared by him with many others) "of Nazareth" (a this-worldly point of origin, and an undistinguished one at that), "the crucified one." (This peculiar Greek phrase, also used by Paul in 1 Corinthians 1:23, is the sole characteristic of Jesus' earthly life that is mentioned in the framework of the empty tomb; he is not "the miracle worker," the "Teacher," nor even "the Lover," but only the "crucified.") "He was raised." (Here the verb is in the passive, referring to God's act.)

If we had only the collection of references discussed here, it would never enter our minds to think of Jesus' earthly life in any other way than as that of a thoroughly human person, differing from ourselves only in the quality of his obedience to God and in love for his fellow human beings.

Paul and the Early Christian Kenosis Christology

The early church prior to Mark used a great number of images with which to picture the salvation event in Christ. These can be divided into two basic categories, depending on how they picture the earthly life of Jesus. The first category, which depicts Jesus' life as filled with divine power, is called epiphany ("manifestation") Christology and comes to expression in the miracle stories discussed in chapter 1. The second, which pictures Jesus' life as utterly human, and thus "empty" of the divine power, is called "kenosis" Christology, from the Greek word *kenoo* meaning "to empty," used by Paul in Philippians 2:7. Mark invented neither one, but found both already used in the church for a generation before him.

In technical discussions of Christology, "kenosis" is used only for the three-stage manner of picturing the Christ-event in which the pre-existent divine Christ "emptied" himself of his divine power when he became human, then was restored to divine status at the resurrection. In this discussion I am using "kenosis" more loosely to refer to all those ways the early Christians thought of Jesus in which his life was *empty* of the divine power, whether thought of in connection with pre-existence or not.

The oldest statement of the Christian faith in the New Testament is expressed in terms of kenosis Christology. In the course of writing a letter to the Corinthians, Paul quotes the early Christian creed which was delivered to him, presumably at the time of his conversion, which he had passed on to the Corinthians as a summary of the Christian message. The tightly structured creedal statement is as follows:

> That Christ died for our sins according to the scriptures, that he was buried, that he was raised on the third day in accordance with the scriptures, and that he appeared to Cephas, then to the twelve (1 Corinthians 15:3-5).

Scholars are agreed that this statement of the church's faith goes back to the earliest days of the church. We should note that it concentrates entirely on the death-resurrection of Jesus as the decisive event in which God's saving act is located. Nothing at all is said of Jesus' *life,* what kind of person he was, etc. In this way of conceptualizing it, God was active in the Jesus-event, but he was active at the *extremity* of Jesus' life, rather than in its midst.

This was also expressed in another creedal statement which was already traditional when Paul wrote the letter to the Romans, and which he quotes in the opening lines (1:3). Paul refers to the gospel (same word as in 1 Corinthians 15:1) concerning God's Son,

> who was descended from David according to the flesh and designated Son of God in power according to the Spirit of holiness by his resurrection from the dead (Romans 1:3).

Like 1 Corinthians 15:3-5, this creed too locates the mighty act of God for our salvation in the resurrection event, not within the earthly life of Jesus. The epiphany Christology had compressed the whole of God's act in Christ into a single picture, a one-stage Christology in which Jesus' divinity threatened to swallow up his humanity. But here we have a kind of two-stage Christology: first the human being, Jesus, a member of this world of flesh and blood by his descent from David. Then the saving "power" of God is revealed when God raises Jesus from the dead and makes him to be his Son.

The type of Christology found in these two early Christian creeds expresses both the human and divine elements with reference to Jesus but it handles them chronologically: first the weakness and humanity, then, at the resurrection, the power and divinity. Other New Testament traditions also think of the Christ-event in these terms. In Acts 2:36, for example, Luke portrays Peter as preaching, "God has made him both Lord and Christ, this Jesus whom you crucified." Although Luke's own way of thinking about the Christ-event is not limited to this conception, he has preserved an early Christian tradition which understands Jesus to have become the Christ, the Lord, at his resurrection just as Romans 1:3 declares that he became the Son of God then. In Paul's sermon in Acts 13:16-47, the resurrection is the turning point when Jesus is "begotten" as the Son of God (v. 33).

We should remember that the formulators of these early Christian confessions had not read the Gospels. We may sometimes be misled by the arrangement of our New Testament to suppose that, because we have already read the Gospels when we read these materials, those who first formulated the materials in Acts and Paul's letters had also done so. Having already conditioned ourselves by our reading of the Gospels to think of the life of Jesus as filled with miracles, we may unconsciously read this picture into such "later" statements in the New Testament as 1 Corinthians 15:3-5; Romans 1:3; and Acts 2:36. But these "later" statements were in fact composed before our Gospels! Although some authors of the epistolary (=letter) and creedal material in the New Testament may have known some traditions that later became part of our Gospels, there were no Gospels yet, and no one could have assumed that the "divine man" of the miracle stories in the Gospels was the normative Christian picture of the life of Jesus. The evidence is rather that several streams of early Christian tradition which found their way into our New Testament were not interested in the "life of Jesus," for they did not locate

God's act within the incidents of his life but in the death-resurrection event by which the man Jesus was exalted to be the Christ, the Lord, the Son of God.

Some early Christians saw that this Christological two-stage drama had an inherent danger in it—that of making it seem that God simply picked a man, though no doubt a good one, and "adopted" him at the resurrection. But this danger was avoided by yet another pattern which also developed very early, a three-stage drama which pictured: (1) the pre-existence of the divine Son of God before his coming to earth; (2) the divesting himself of his divine powers in order to live on earth as a man; (3) an exaltation at his death and resurrection which returned him to his former glory.

Philippians 2:5-11

This three-stage pattern is classically expressed in the early Christian hymn which Paul quotes in Philippians 2:5-11. The drama begins in the heavenly world, Act One picturing "Christ Jesus . . . in the form of God" (v. 6). In this song, the Jesus-story does not begin at Jordan or at Bethlehem but in the eternal world of God. Christ was "fully divine" in the sense that he belonged to the divine world rather than the human one, but (unlike Adam-and-Eve humanity in the garden, Genesis 3:5-6) he did not grasp at being equal to God. Unlike pagan myths, the song does not elaborate the scene in the heavenly world but, having established that the Jesus-story originates there, moves quickly to this world.

In Act Two, Christ enters this world in the form of a man. The same word "form" *(morphe)* is used here in v. 7 to describe his human existence as had been used in v. 6 of his divine pre-existence, a word which means not mere external form but "reality." The hymn pictures his human existence in this world as being just as real as his divine existence in the heavenly world. This is emphasized by the key work *ekenosen,* translated [he] emptied himself" (v. 7). The Christ who had participated in the divine life did not hold to his divinity but divested himself of his divine powers and entered this world as a "servant." (*The Living Bible's* use of the word "disguise" at this point is patently heretical.)

The word "servant" is *doulos,* commonly translated "slave," and refers not just to Jesus' humble attitude while on this earth but to the human condition in general. From the point of view of the hymn's author, to be a human being is to be in slavery to the powers that rule this world and dominate life. While he thought of the "principalities and powers" as mythological (Romans 8:38-39; Galatians 4:3; Ephesians 6:12), we understand the phrase to refer to powers, sometimes demonic, to which every human life is subject. There is a sense in which to be a human being is to be a victim, a powerless slave, to the "givens" of life. This song affirms that Jesus entered into this human bondage.

One might think of human life as lived in a deep canyon completely surrounded with sheer walls, a valley with both joys and sorrows, good and evil, justice and injustice, love and hate. But everyone in the canyon lives under the same limitations and cannot escape to some other world of unmixed bliss. A powerful figure stands on the rim of the canyon, himself untainted by the ambiguities and limitations of life in the valley below. If he

56

decides to descend, he must let go of the rope when he reaches the bottom and share the life of the inhabitants of the canyon. He cannot get back up by his own power but, like everyone else in the valley, is dependent on some power from beyond the valley itself to lift him out. In the song, Christ does enter the canyon of human existence, becomes a slave to the powers that dominate us, and lives a life obedient to God until his death. (Again, the contrast with Adam must leap to our minds [Genesis 3:1-24; cf. Romans 5:12-21].)

Act Three is the cross-resurrection event by which Jesus is exalted by God back to his former status—even beyond—and is given the name ("Lord") that is above every name, having become Lord of the whole creation. Here we have a way of talking about both Jesus' divinity and his humanity, a way which handles it chronologically: divinity/humanity/divinity or power/weakness/power. The act of God-in-Christ is thought of as a U-shaped event, in which divinity is manifested at the extremities. The bottom segment of the "U," the thirty years of the earthly life of Jesus, is characterized by weakness. (See Diagram 5.)

This hymn was not composed by Paul but was part of the tradition (and worship) of the pre-Pauline Hellenistic church. Paul adopts it and uses it because it expresses his own understanding of the Christ-event, the theology which was the basis for his pastoral ministry. Paul does not include it in Philippians as an interesting bit of speculation but as an element in his pastoral counseling of the Philippian congregation on a practical issue. In the midst of his exhortations for congregational unity, apparently attempting to squelch a growing divisiveness or a quarrel in the Philippian church, Paul urges his readers to abandon petty self-interest and to live their lives in behalf of others. Jesus is brought into the discussion as the supreme example to be followed.

It is very important to note that Paul does not lift out as an example some appropriate incident from the *earthly* life of Jesus, such as the washing of the disciples' feet (John 13). Jesus, the humble servant of others, is depicted in terms of a cosmic drama. It is not the humble attitude of the earthly Jesus, who girds his body with a towel and serves his fellows, which awes Paul and calls him to discipleship, but rather that there *was* an earthly Jesus, that the divine Son of God abandoned his divinity and had a body at all. When Paul wants to say "Be like Jesus," he thinks of the love of the divine Christ who came to earth as the human Jesus, not of anything in particular that the earthly Jesus did. *That* there was an earthly Jesus, not *what* he was, is the emphasis of Paul's gospel. So also, when Paul urges the Corinthian church to give sacrificially for the contribution for "the poor" in the Jerusalem church and wants to use Jesus as a model of such sacrifice, he does not refer to any deed of the earthly Jesus but portrays the sacrifice made by the heavenly Christ in coming into this world for our sakes (2 Corinthians 8:9).

Various estimates have been given by scholars as to how much Paul in fact knew about the historical Jesus. He was, of course, not an eyewitness to Jesus' ministry, and had been converted not by contact with the historical Jesus but by encounters with the exalted Lord sometime after

Diagram 5

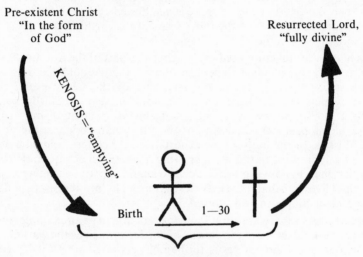

Pre-existent Christ
"In the form
of God"

Resurrected Lord,
"fully divine"

KENOSIS = "emptying"

Birth   1—30

The "days of his flesh,"
the human life of Jesus
empty of the divine power,
"crucified in weakness"

Jesus' death and resurrection (Galatians 1:11—2:10; Acts 9:1-30). He certainly had considerable opportunity to learn "the facts" about Jesus' earthly ministry from those who had been there and from the stories about him that circulated in the Christian tradition (cf. e.g., Galatians 1:18). (Again: Remember that there were as yet no Gospels to read!) But the question of how much Paul *could* have known, or *did* know, about the actual incidents in the life of the human Jesus is somewhat beside the point. Paul's own letters indicate that he had little interest in the details of Jesus' life (e.g., 2 Corinthians 5:14-21, especially v. 16), for it is what God did through Jesus in the cross and resurrection that plays the major role in Paul's theology.

When Paul does refer to the earthly life of Jesus, it is entirely in terms of his humanity. Surprisingly few readers of Paul's letters have noticed that he never once refers to any miraculous act of the earthly Jesus, that he does not give even a hint that he supposed Jesus during his earthly life was capable of extraordinary acts of divine power, or that on the contrary he emphasizes the weakness of the crucified Jesus (1 Corinthians 1:18—2:5; 15:3-5; 2 Corinthians 5:14-21; 13:4; Romans 5:6-21; Philippians 2:5-11). It is important for Paul that there *was* a Jesus who had lived a human life among us, obedient to God, and who had been crucified. This, in the context of Paul's understanding of pre-existence and resurrection, is all that matters, but this minimum is the critical mass which matters supremely. Jesus was no mythical figure for Paul, and could not be so. It was not just the "principle," the "idea" or "ideal" enshrined in the story of Christ's incarnation, human life, and exaltation, that was saving but that it had actually happened, that the act of God took place in a real historical event, embodied in a man who actually lived and died. Paul is representative of early Christianity when he insists that what he has to share is not good advice or helpful theory but good *news* about something that has happened.

But for Paul this life of Jesus in which God acted for our salvation was a human life which shared the weakness and limitations of the human situation in general. Paul does not present any miracles in the life of Jesus. But it is not merely the case that Paul *happened* not to tell any miracle stories about Jesus in the letters that have come down to us. Paul *could* not tell any such stories—there was no place for them in his kenosis Christology.

The Pauline letters, written in the 50s and 60s of the first century, are first-generation writings, and are the oldest documents preserved for us from the early church. The traditional materials they preserve are older still. Thus kenosis Christology was one of the earliest ways of conceptualizing the Christ-event. But when the Gospels began to be written at the end of the first generation, beginning with Mark about A.D. 70, the kenosis model for thinking of Jesus did not die out. Paul had made the epistolary form of writing into a powerful and popular means of expressing the faith, *and it continued in the church alongside the Gospels as an alternative to them.*

Paul's letters were preserved, collected, and circulated, and other letters modeled on them were written. Except for Matthew, Mark, Luke-Acts (two volumes of one literary work) and John, *all the rest of the New*

Testament is in the form of letters, and all the rest of it assumes a kenosis Christology, which is usually made explicit. There are thus in the New Testament two fundamental models for the expression of the faith: the Gospel form, which included the miracle stories, and the letters, which did not. We may look at two more examples of kenosis Christology in the letters.

The Kenosis Christology of Hebrews

The Letter to the Hebrews contains some of the most exalted language with reference to Christ to be found in the New Testament. The first sentence declares that he has been "appointed the heir of all things," that God "created the world" through him, that he "reflects the glory of God and bears the very stamp of his nature, upholding the universe by his word of power," that he has "made purification for sins," and "sat down at the right hand of the Majesty on high" (1:2-4). The picture taken from Psalm 110 of the divine chief priest, seated at the right hand of God as our intercessor until the end of time, is a special favorite of the author. Unlike Paul, the author does not draw back from applying even the word "God" to Christ (1:8). No divine superlative is too exalted to be used of the Eternal Christ, "who is the same yesterday and today and for ever" (13:8).

Yet it must be clearly seen that all this talk of Christ's divinity applies to the pre-existent or post-resurrection Christ. Like Paul, the writer of Hebrews conceives of the drama of salvation in three acts, and talks about Christ's divinity in terms of acts one and three. But the middle act, the earthly career of the man Jesus, is portrayed exclusively in almost embarrassingly human terms.

This is not a grudging concession to reality or the "facts." Since the author conceives Jesus' salvific role primarily in priestly terms, it is important for a priest, in order to function in behalf of those for whose sake he ministers, *to be one of them.* Thus the author emphasizes that "he who sanctifies and these who are sanctified have all one origin" (NEB: "all of one stock"), that he "is not ashamed to call them brethren" (2:11). Since the people for whom his priestly ministry is carried out "share in flesh and blood, he himself likewise partook of the same nature, that through [his own] death he might destroy him who has the power of death, that is, the devil" (2:14).

We might parenthetically note the similarity and the difference between this text and the miracle story in Mark 5. In both cases the demonic power of death is the threat, and in both cases the testimony is given that in Jesus, God has acted to overcome the power of death and set us free to enjoy the fullness of life for which he created us. In Mark 5 this is pictured as the power of Jesus in raising a little girl from the dead; here, it is pictured as the weakness of the earthly Jesus, who is himself given over to death.

In 2:17, the author states without qualification that in order to fulfill his priestly ministry, Jesus "had to be made like his brethren in every respect," which includes suffering, being tempted (2:18), even being *made perfect* by what he suffered (2:10, 5:8-9), praying "with loud cries and tears" (5:7, cf.

the Gethsemane scene in Mark 14:32-36, and above). "For we have not a high priest who is unable to sympathize with our weaknesses, but one who in every respect" has experienced what we experience (this is the better translation of *peirazo,* "tempt," here; 4:15), one who, like the chief priest of the Old Testament who is used for the model here, is "himself beset with weakness" (5:2). Like Paul, the author uses the word "weakness" to characterize the earthly career of Jesus, and like Paul, he admits of only one exception to his being completely like us: He was completely obedient to the will of God (4:15).

All this is clearly expressed in one passage, 2:5-9. Like the later Arians at the time of the trinitarian controversy in the fourth century, the recipients of the letter were inclined to think of Jesus as somehow more than a man but less than fully divine—something like an angel. A pretty high status, we might think, but it was not adequate for the author of Hebrews, or for any other New Testament author, or for those church fathers who, in our behalf, hammered out the doctrine of the trinity amidst the abstruse controversies of the fourth century.

What was at issue in those arguments—petty-sounding though they may be to us—is whether or not that which is revealed in Jesus is really ultimate. Although the battle was fought in terms of the "nature" of Jesus, the issue was not what the person of Jesus was made of, or whether it had existed eternally, but whether or not the revelation that happened in Jesus was the revelation of *God* or of something else. The Christian claim is not that some interesting occult information from the "other side" was revealed by Jesus but that the ultimate nature of history and the universe, that is, God, is revealed in him. However high we may conceive his "nature" to be, we have still missed the claim of the New Testament and the early church if we suppose that sometime, somewhere, apart from Jesus we might learn what life and the world are *really* all about. This latter is the implication of thinking of Christ in only "angelic," "quasi-divine" terms, and is why the church later used terms like "Very God of Very God" of him. This is why the author of Hebrews is constrained to begin his argument by insisting that Jesus was superior to angels, that only terms like "Son of God" and even "God" are adequate when speaking of him (1:4—2:5). It is precisely this one, in the author's theology, of whom no predicate is too high, who "for a little while" became lower than the angels and lived as a human being (2:9).

The author of Hebrews has found in Psalm 8 the words which express his understanding of the Christ-event. When we turn to this psalm, we may be bothered to discover that the quotation in Hebrews has significant differences from the way the psalm appears in our Old Testament, and indeed Hebrews' point seems to rest precisely on words that are different from the version of Psalm 8 in our Bible. This is not an unusual state of affairs to discover when comparing our text of the Old Testament with the many places where it is quoted in the New Testament. Of the five key scriptural quotations with which Matthew begins his Gospel, for instance, not one is exactly the same in Matthew as in our text of the Old Testament, and three have substantial differences. We may use this instance in

Hebrews as an opportunity to explore briefly the general principles which govern the New Testament's usage of the Old. There are, of course, variations among the individual writers, but the following two points will be found to apply generally.

(1) The early church understood the history of Jesus and its own history in continuity with that of the Old Testament and as the climax and fulfillment of it. This accounts for the extensive use of Old Testament phraseology in describing the story of Jesus and the Christian life, even when the Old Testament is not quoted directly. It also accounts for the willingness of New Testament authors to alter the Old Testament text in ways that may seem arbitrary or even dishonest to us, in order to make the Old Testament promise and the New Testament fulfillment match more perfectly. But New Testament authors are not to be charged with a lapse of integrity at this point. They were the eschatological community, which read the scripture already convinced that it was fulfilled in Jesus and in their own history. The Old Testament functioned not as *proof* of their claim but as illustration of it. The fulfillment had primacy over the promise, and in this view nothing was violated if the texts containing the promise were adjusted to point more clearly to the fulfillment.

In this the early church functioned exactly like their contemporaries, the Jewish community at Qumran, whose library was found at the Dead Sea and who were convinced that they were the eschatological community of fulfillment. They interpreted the Old Testament to refer to themselves with the same freedom that the early Christians interpreted it of Jesus and the church. The question we are met with in each instance is not whether liberties were taken with the text (which is obvious) but whether the eschatological claim expressed therein is true. The issue is not whether the Old Testament predicted the events of Jesus' life, or whether the church altered its texts to make it appear that this was the case, but whether the early church's faith which came to expression in this use of the Old Testament, the faith that God's purpose as declared in the Scriptures is fulfilled in Jesus, is true or not.

(2) The early church was able to do this more easily because it used the Greek Septuagint (abbreviated LXX) as its Bible. The Old Testament had been written in Hebrew and (a small amount of) Aramaic, a related Semitic language. But by the time the New Testament documents were written, Christianity had become a predominantly Gentile religion whose language was Greek, so that most early Christians did not read the Scriptures in the languages in which they were written but in the LXX translation made for Greek-speaking Jews from the third to the first centuries before Christ. As is the case with translations in general, the LXX translation did not always express the thought of the original, or what the translator took to be the thought of the original, in precisely the form in which the original author had written it. And while our English Old Testament is translated from the oldest and most reliable texts we have, the LXX was sometimes translated from texts which were certainly older and, in some instances, better preserved than the original. Thus a considerable amount of the difference between our Old Testament may be accounted for by the fact that our Old

Testament is a translation of the Hebrew text, while the New Testament authors used a Greek translation of this, which was sometimes based on Hebrew texts which differ from the ones we use.

Another possibility is that the writer of Hebrews may have adjusted his translation to bring out the meaning more clearly to his own situation. This is the explanation in the case before us, Hebrews 2:5-9 and its use of Psalm 8. The author of Hebrews is using the LXX of Psalm 8, which had rendered the Hebrew word for "God" (cf. RSV) as "angels." (The LXX had good reasons for doing this; see below.) The LXX also translated the Hebrew expression rendered in English as "little lower" by a Greek expression which can mean "little lower" (degree) or "little while lower" (time). By virtue of this phenomenon of translation, the author of Hebrews was able to find in his Greek Bible a text which seemed to express his understanding of the Christ-event perfectly! Psalm 8:5 in the Hebrew text had originally expressed the splendor of humanity as the creation of God. Man stands tall on the earth, above the other creatures over whom he is given dominion. Indeed, he is "little less than God" (or perhaps the Hebrew is better expressed in English as "a god," i.e. "a divine being," which is why the LXX properly translated it as "angels").

But the author of Hebrews sees in his Greek translation something said about the Son of Man. (The original psalm referred to man in general, as the parallelism of man/son of man in v. 4 shows.) But "Son of Man" was an early Christian title for Jesus, and in Greek-speaking Christianity the odd-sounding phrase was no longer recognized as a Hebrew idiom for "human being" in general, so our author takes it as a clue that the psalm is about *the* Son of Man, Jesus, and interprets it accordingly. Thus a psalm about humanity in general is seen by the author of Hebrews to be a psalm about Jesus. Taking the ambiguous Greek phrase as meaning "for a little while," the author understands the psalm to be testifying to "Jesus, who for a little while was made lower than the angels" (2:9). Like the framers of the Nicene Creed, the writer of Hebrews believed that Christ was "fully divine" and that he was the fulfillment of God's purpose as expressed in the Scriptures. Nevertheless, he expressed this in the kenotic Christology, in which the earthly life of Jesus was utterly human. As in the case of Paul, the important things about Jesus' earthly life were that it really happened, that it was characterized by full obedience to God, and that it ended in death on the cross. Not only are miracles not recounted; there is no place for them in such a rendering of Jesus' life.

The Kenosis Christology of Revelation

The Book of Revelation is also a letter. Its content is almost completely composed of apocalyptic material, that is, revealed pictures of the triumph of God over evil at the end of history, a common literary form in the Judaism of the first century which was adopted by the early church. But though filled with apocalyptic content, the form of the book is a pastoral letter from a Christian leader to seven churches in the province of Asia who were facing the threat of persecution.

The book is almost entirely devoted to pictures of what Jesus will do as the divine Son of God when he returns to execute God's work at the End, an event which the author believes to be very near (1:1, 3; 2:16; 3:11; etc.). Revelation's Christology too is structured in terms of the three-act drama. But we now see that the third act of the Christological drama has three scenes: (1) the resurrection-exaltation of Jesus, in the writer's past; (2) the "session" of the exalted Christ at the right hand of God, in the writer's present; and (3) the return of the heavenly Lord at the end of history. These are all ways of affirming the post-resurrection divinity of Christ, not ways of talking about his human life. These elements are all present, but with different emphases, in each of the New Testament writers we have studied this far. Paul's primary emphasis is on the significance of the resurrection, while Hebrews stresses the present priestly activity of the risen Christ "since he always lives to make intercession for them" (Hebrews 7:25). But Revelation's emphasis is on the final scene of the final act, the return of Jesus in glory to establish fully God's kingdom throughout the universe.

There is no question but that John affirms that the risen Jesus is fully divine, for he pictures Jesus' sharing the divine life as fully as imagery and vocabulary will permit it to be expressed. He is the "first-born of the dead, and the ruler of kings on earth" (1:5). In 1:13-16, he is portrayed as a gigantic figure who holds the stars in his hands, spanning the cosmos, who is present with his churches in the same way God is present. He is described with the same symbolic expressions used in Daniel 7:9ff. of God himself, suggesting God's own kingly power, wisdom, eternity, and awesome holiness. John responds in terror to this vision of the exalted Christ, just as Isaiah did to his vision of God (Isaiah 6:5). He is repeatedly associated with God's own reign and is practically identified with the Almighty who sits upon the throne (7:10; 21:22; 22:1; etc.). He is the one who shall come at the end of history as the Mighty Warrior to destroy evil and bring in God's kingdom (19:11-16 and the remainder of the book). This heavenly Christ of Act Three is the "First" as well as the "Last" (1:17), that is, he pre-existed with God in Act One, "from the foundation of the world" and was the "beginning of God's creation" (3:14).

The bizarre symbolism which pictures the dramatic return of Jesus at the end of history has usually attracted so much attention to itself (either in fascination or revulsion) that it is rarely noticed that this divine figure who returns at the denouement in Act Three is in continuity with, in fact is identified with, the earthly Jesus of Act Two. Yet this is the crucial thing about Revelation's theology, the only thing which keeps Revelation from being just another of the Jewish apocalypses promising that, however tough things may be now, God will soon send a mighty heavenly figure to smash our enemies and restore us to our rightful place. Revelation does indeed use this imagery without restraint, so that some Christians have seen Revelation as a sub-Christian book which only longs for the eschatological revenge which shall be meted out to God's (our) enemies when the great Day finally arrives.

But Revelation is not, as Rudolf Bultmann thought, merely "weakly christianized Judaism."[17] In it apocalyptic has undergone a fundamental transformation, for it declares that the traditional Mighty Warrior who shall descend from heaven at the end of time is none other than Jesus of Nazareth, who has already revealed his character, and the character of God, during his life on earth. And what does Revelation tell us of the earthly life of Jesus? That he was born (12:5) of the seed of David (22:16), and that he died (1:5, 7, 18; etc.). The principal title for Jesus throughout is: the Lamb, by which is meant specifically the slaughtered lamb, the weak one who becomes the victim at the hands of the strong, the one who by his very weakness receives the sin of others and delivers them from it (5:6, 8, 12, 13; 6:1, 16; 7:9, 10, 14, 17; 8:1; 12:11; 13:8; 14:1, 4, 10; 15:3; 17:14; 19:7, 9; 21:9, 14, 22, 23; 22:1, 3). The portrayal of the *earthly* life of Jesus presented by Revelation is that of the weakness and vulnerability of the Lamb of God, who has no miraculous power by which he overcomes his enemies. It is the kenosis Christology within which Jesus works no miracle.

There is no more mind-wrenching imagery in literature than in the key scene in 5:1-14. The setting is the heavenly throne-room, the "Mission Control" of the universe. The Almighty, whose purposes are a mystery, sits upon the throne. In his hand is the book which contains the answers that a persecuted church needs and longs for, the what and why of our suffering existence. Suffering itself is not the curse; it is the meaninglessness of it which is unbearable. As a Jewish apocalyptist, a contemporary of John, writes:

> It would be better for us not to be here than to come here and live in
> ungodliness, and to suffer and not understand why (2 Esdras 4:12).

There *are* answers. But we do not have them. The answers are in the book in the hand of God, and it is a sealed book, a book which "no one in heaven or on earth or under the earth was able to open . . . or to look into it" (5:3). John weeps for all of us that life and suffering must remain a mystery (5:4).

But then comes the good news: "Weep not; lo, the Lion of the tribe of Judah, the Root of David, has conquered, so that he can open the scroll and its seven seals" (5:5). Here is the affirmation of the often-expressed, often-disappointed Jewish hope of the Lion-like Messiah, the deliverer that God would finally send to devour the enemies of life and reveal the divine purpose in it all. So far, it is the same Jewish apocalyptic hope, which we may either try to believe again or turn away from in disgust, having been disappointed too many times already. But if we look at the figure to which John is pointing, the one who will take the sealed book from the hand of God and with sovereign authority open its seals and preside over the completion of God's purpose in history, if one last time we muster up the faith or credulity to join in the cheers for the Lion that God has finally sent, we behold—a lamb. His "conquering" means that he was crucified (3:21). His power is entirely the power of suffering love. The book of destiny, the future of the world, is in the hands of this one.

This is what make Revelation Christian. The old images are there without restraint, violent images of the divine Messiah who comes at the End and brings in God's kingdom by ruthless power. But the images are filled with a new content. The Messiah of Act Three is none other than the

65

Jesus of Act Two. Revelation, like all the New Testament, dares to ask us to believe that the Messiah has come, that he is Jesus of Nazareth, the crucified one.

One reason so many thinking, sensitive Christians have been alienated from the message of Revelation is that it has been practically taken over by "pop-eschatology," which has missed its central message. For in this doctrine, the Jesus who is expected to return soon is a different Jesus from the Jesus of suffering love, the one who turned the other cheek, whose only power against evil was his lovingly accepting its consequences, who would win by love or not at all. The typical pop-eschatology doctrine is that God tried weakness and love during Jesus' "first coming," but that, at the "second coming," those who wouldn't accept love will get terribly violent consequences. In this view, God's love revealed in Jesus' "first coming" was only a temporary strategy, but his ultimate nature is vindictive violence to be revealed at the "second coming." In pop-eschatology, the Jesus who "comes back" is a different Jesus than the one we met in his A.D. 30 history. In fact, it is not *Jesus* at all but the old Jewish apocalyptic Messiah, not changed one whit by his encounter with the crucified Jesus of Nazareth, whose name he falsely wears.

Revelation has radically Christianized this traditional apocalyptic view. The Act Three drama will be played out. As Reinhold Niebuhr, no sentimentalist, declared: "History is to have a worthy conclusion."[18] The divine Christ, acting with the power of God Almighty, will bring all things under his rule. But *what* that power is has already been revealed in Act Two, in the love of Jesus lived out in human weakness culminating in a cross. It is this, not the weird imagery or complicated symbolism, which makes Revelation so hard to believe. We still identify the Messiah with the Lion, whether to rally around his banner or to turn away. But in Jesus, God has revealed his ultimate nature, not a passing whim or provisional strategy. The love that is willing to suffer at the hands of evil knows that it will win in the end, because it is the ultimate power in the universe, the power of God himself. God has revealed in Jesus the power by which he will finally subject all things to himself. There is no "Plan B."

* * *

In the three examples of the epistolary literature which we have chosen (Paul, Hebrews, Revelation), we have seen three variations on the same kenotic pattern. The deity of Christ is affirmed in each case by picturing the glorious power of the pre-existent and post-resurrection Christ, while his life "in the days of his flesh" (Hebrews 5:7) is characterized entirely by human weakness. We will now see that this picture of the life of Jesus is also reflected in some elements of the material which came to the authors of the Synoptic Gospels.

Kenosis Christology in the Pre-Synoptic Tradition

We have already pointed out the several places in Mark which indicate that the human life of Jesus was devoid of divine power (see pp. 49-54 above). While some of this is of Mark's own composition, other elements were in the pre-Markan tradition (e.g., 8:11-12). It is also the case that some traditional material which came to Matthew and Luke, previously circulated as individual units in the church prior to being incorporated in the written Gospels, conceived the life of Jesus in kenotic terms.

Matthew 1-2; Luke 1-2

We may first think of the stories of Jesus' birth found in Matthew and Luke, and the one scene from his childhood in Luke 2:41-52. What is more helpless and vulnerable than a newborn baby? In the Christmas story our attention is usually drawn so quickly to the miraculous nature of Jesus' conception that we may fail to notice the shocking character of telling of the *birth* of a "divine being" at *all.* For how could the Son of God live in the fragile weakness of babyhood? If the stories may seem to us to have been intended to display the miraculous power involved in Jesus' birth, it was the power of *God,* and no question is ever raised but that the baby Jesus himself shares the weakness and vulnerability of all human children. One group of early Christians, Marcion and his many followers, were so concerned about the birth stories compromising the divinity of Jesus that they rejected them as false, explaining that Jesus had arrived on this earth from the divine world full grown.[19] Though Marcion did this as an attempt to safeguard the divinity of Jesus, his interpretations and writings were considered heretical by mainstream Christianity.

But even those who accept the stories as valid witnesses to the meaning of the Christ-event may suppose that they point to the divinity of Jesus rather than his humanity. Since these are stories of the birth and childhood of the Son of God, who is divine not just from the time of his baptism and reception of the divine Spirit but from the time of his miraculous conception by the Spirit onwards, should we not first be struck by the remarkable absence of powerful divine feats performed by the divine child himself? It would seem that the logical (not to say bio-logical) inference from a conception by divine power should be an extraordinary child filled with divine power. There were, in fact, numerous Gospels written in the early church which drew precisely this inference, picturing a little-boy Jesus who confounded his teachers and terrorized the playground by his miraculous feats.

Some examples:[20]

At Jesus' birth, a great light shone around the cave where Mary was in labor, then gradually withdrew itself as the young child appeared. When the baby was born, "it went and took the breast of its mother Mary" at its own initiative (*Book of James,* 19:2).

When Salome, a passerby, doubted that the baby had been born of a virgin, the midwife invited her to give Mary a physical examination to establish that her virginity was intact even after the birth. When Salome did so, her finger began to burn but was healed by touching the baby Jesus (*Book of James,* 19:3—20:4).

At the age of five, the boy Jesus was playing on the Sabbath and had made some sparrows from clay. When he was criticized for profaning the Sabbath, he clapped his hands and the clay sparrows became alive and flew away, thereby destroying the evidence that he had "worked" on the Sabbath (*Infancy Gospel of Thomas,* 2:1-4).

When Jesus is taken to school, he embarrasses and confounds the teacher, for he not only already knows the (Greek!) alphabet with which the hapless instructor begins but also expounds the mystical meanings of the letters in accord with later Gnostic instruction. The awestruck teacher responds to the child as to a god: "Woe is me, I am forced into a quandary, wretch that I am; I have brought shame to myself in drawing to myself this child. Take him away, therefore, I beseech you, brother Joseph. I cannot endure the severity of his look, I cannot make out his speech at all. This child is not earth-born; he can tame even fire. Perhaps he was begotten even before the creation of the world" (*Infancy Gospel of Thomas,* 6:1—7:2).

The superboy Jesus was the terror of the neighborhood, sometimes blinding or maiming children who disagreed with him, on some occasions even killing them—but then he also raised them from the dead (*Infancy Gospel of Thomas,* 4:1; 5:1; 9:1-3). But he also sometimes used his powers for constructive purposes, healing his brother James of snakebite (*Infancy Gospel of Thomas,* 16:1-2).

In contrast to all this, Matthew is discreetly silent about Jesus' life between the time of his birth and the beginning of his ministry, while Luke includes only the one scene in which Jesus conspicuously works no miracle. The boy Jesus in Luke has a normal human development, growing up in obedience to Mary and Joseph, gradually increasing his knowledge, a precociously sensitive and religious child but no superboy, a child who works no miracle (Luke 2:41-52).

Matthew 4:1-11; Luke 4:1-13

This story of Jesus' three-fold temptation by Satan in the wilderness is not in Mark but is contained in Matthew and Luke in almost identical wording, except that one or the other of them has rearranged the order of the last two temptations. This means that the story was part of the common source used by Matthew and Luke, an early collection of individual sayings of Jesus called "Q" (abbreviation of *Quelle,* "source") by scholars. In the oral tradition the story originally circulated separately, apart from any narrative context, and made its witness to the meaning of the Christ-event without any connection to other stories and sayings in the tradition.

The story is told from the point of view within the Christian faith and assumes faith in Jesus as the Son of God (Matthew 4:2, 6 and parallels). The devil tempts Jesus to prove (also to himself?) that he is the Son of God by demonstrating the divine power inherent in this claim, by turning stones to bread (thereby solving the world's hunger problem), jumping off the temple (thereby proving to the masses that he was what he claimed to be, a demonstration very like "come down from the cross"), and by launching a campaign of world conquest, using methods originating from the devil and in effect in service to him. The story apparently assumes that Jesus in fact *could* have done all this; i.e., it is narrated within the logical framework of the epiphany Christology. But it is just as clear that the story denies that Jesus' life *was* like this. The story's point is that if Jesus had lived his life like this, it would have been a demonic betrayal of his mission in the world as Son of God, not a proof of it.

This original point of the story, so obvious when taken by itself, has been obscured for most readers by its present context within the narratives of Matthew and Luke, where, in both cases, Jesus does proceed to a ministry which is full of miraculous power in behalf of others. Thus the typical explanation of this story has been that Jesus refused to use his miraculous power selfishly, though he could and did use it for others. Although this is predominantly the case, this explanation is not wholly satisfactory, since both Matthew (17:24-27) and Luke (4:28-30) do provide cases in which Jesus' divine power is used for his own benefit. But we are presently concerned to examine the forms of Christological confession prior to the origination of the Gospel form, while the individual units of tradition circulated separately. So, although the interpretation of the story in its Matthean and Lukan setting is a necessary and important task, we must first look at the message of the story taken by itself.

The story obviously has to do not with Jesus' personal comfort during the six weeks in the desert but with *the nature of his ministry.* Bread, circuses, and visions of world conquest are means of winning others to one's cause, not items of personal convenience. Could it be any clearer that this story considers the "divine man" style of ministry a demonic betrayal of the mission of the Son of God, a temptation which Jesus resisted, so that however much divine power the earthly Jesus "could" have exercised, in fact he did not? To explain "Son of God" in terms of working miracles is to speak with the voice of Satan. Like the birth stories, the temptation stories picture the meaning of the gospel in a scene within the confines of the earthly life of Jesus, and thus resemble the epiphany Christology. But, also like the birth stories, the temptation stories have ways other than the miraculous of affirming that this earthly life was the life of the Son of God. In this they are like the kenosis Christology. Like Paul, Hebrews, and the kenosis Christology in general, the temptation stories affirm that the earthly life of Jesus differed from our own only in that he was truly obedient to God.

Matthew 12:38-42; Luke 11:29-32

We have already discussed the tradition in which Jesus refuses to work miracles and categorically declares that no sign will be given to his generation, an element of the pre-Markan tradition which Mark included in his Gospel (Mark 8:11-13, cf. above, p. 52). Here we need only point out that Q also contained a variation of this tradition, which declares that the "Sign of Jonah" will be the only sign given to Jesus' generation. Jonah performed no miracles. Matthew interprets the Jonah reference to mean the resurrection of Jesus; Luke apparently understands the preaching of Jesus to be the point of resemblance to Jonah. In either case, the ministry is declared to be empty of miraculous signs.

* * *

The emphasis of the early Christian kenosis Christology on Jesus' humanity was preserved and extended by some second-century streams of Jewish Christianity. Ebionism, a Jewish-Christian sect considered heretical by developing Catholic Christianity, and the Jewish-Christian group behind the Clementine *Recognitions* and *Homilies* (which may also be an Ebionite group), considered it an article of faith that Jesus was a man, not a divine being. Although they believed that Jesus had worked miracles, they insisted that he did this as a man endowed with God's power, as did the Old Testament prophets, not as a divine being. To express their faith in Jesus' humanity, they rejected the stories of Jesus' virgin birth and did not in any sense consider the earthly Jesus to be the Son of God. Like the Old Testament prophets, Jesus was inspired by the Spirit, which he received at his baptism, to properly interpret the will of God. He was the True Prophet, the last and greatest of the prophetic line. He truly died a human death. After his death, he was exalted by God to be a heavenly being, a kind of angel, and he will come back at the end of history as the Son of Man. This final development of kenotic Christology was rightly condemned by the church as heretical, for it affirmed Jesus' humanity only at the expense of his divinity. Just as epiphany Christology developed into the heresy of Docetism in the second century, kenosis Christology developed into the heresy of Ebionism.[21]

In sum, we see that the kenosis Christology is the obverse of epiphany Christology, both in its picture of the life of Jesus and in the logical inferences from this picture. Epiphany Christology pictures the life of Jesus as a manifestation of the superhuman power of God; kenosis Christology pictures the life of Jesus as an utterly human identification with the weakness of humanity. The logic of one says "If he was truly divine, his earthly life couldn't have been human"; the logic of the other says "If he were truly human, his earthly life couldn't have been divine." These two Christologies have the same logical pattern; both operate within the same kind of logic. And they both have the same foundational affirmation: "God has acted in Jesus Christ for our salvation." But in each case the *way* this is expressed seems to exclude the other. The result was that, although the early church expressed its faith in both kinds of Christology, these Christologies did not peacefully coexist. Each saw the other as the opponent of faith.

For Further Reading

Fuller, Reginald H., *The Foundations of New Testament Christology.* Charles Scribner's Sons, 1965.

Hengel, Martin, *Crucifixion: In the Ancient World and the Folly of the Message of the Cross.* Fortress Press, 1977.

Kelber, Werner, ed., *The Passion in Mark: Studies in Mark 14–16.* Fortress Press, 1976.

Moltmann, Jürgen, *The Crucified God.* Harper & Row, 1974.

Pollard, T. E., *Fullness of Humanity: Christ's Humanness and Ours.* Almond Press, 1982.

Robinson, John A. T., *The Human Face of God.* Westminster Press, 1973.

Schillebeeckx, Edward, *Jesus: An Experiment in Christology.* Crossroad, 1981.

3

The Gospel as Gospel

The Struggle of Two Opposing Christologies
Mark Affirms Both Christologies
Messianic Secret, Gospel Form, and Christological
*   Language*

The Struggle of Two Opposing Christologies

The early church produced literature which advocated a pure epiphany Christology—the docetic "Gospels" and "Acts" which were excluded from the New Testament canon. But epiphany Christology was represented not only by these late developments. We know that, very early in the life of the church, there were advocates of the "divine man" way of proclaiming the gospel, for the literary results of their preaching are found in the New Testament miracle stories and they are met as the opponents of Paul's kenosis Christology in the epistles.

In Paul's correspondence with the Corinthian church, for example, we may overhear a heated, sometimes vicious debate between proponents of the two opposed ways of understanding Jesus. Paul had founded the Corinthian church and had emphasized the gospel centered in the cross and resurrection of Jesus and a corresponding style of Christian life. Apparently the report which Paul had heard of developments among the Corinthians since his departure made him suspect that they were in danger of substituting a different understanding of the Christ-event for the one he had given them. In a long and intense passage not in response to their question but volunteered on his own initiative, Paul insists that the gospel is centered on the act of God in the humiliation and weakness of the crucified Jesus (1 Corinthians 1:18—2:5). The weakness of Jesus on the cross was not simply the prelude to the divine power in the resurrection but was itself the power of God (1:17-18). In Paul's view, to replace this picture of a "weak" Jesus with that of a "strong" one only appears on the surface to affirm the power of God. In fact, it surrenders the gospel to a pagan understanding of power, and loses the real power of God. Paul already sensed this as a danger when he wrote 1 Corinthians.

This is probably the clue to the correct understanding of the strange event that had happened in the Corinthian worship which is alluded to in 12:3—someone supposedly overwhelmed with the Spirit had uttered a curse on Jesus. This is an expression of the developing "divine man" Christology at Corinth, one which disdained the weakness of the crucified Jesus. It distinguished this from the power of the heavenly spiritual Christ and considered the latter to be the proper object of the Christian's faith. It was in the name of the "divinity of Christ" that the human *Jesus* was cursed. (We should not think of obscenity or slang here but of "curse" in the liturgical sense of pronouncing anathema on the object of the divine wrath.) One thinks of the Gnostic documents which express laughter at the idea that the spiritual Christ could be crucified (cf. p. 45 above).

The development of this view of Christ was given fresh impetus by the arrival at Corinth of missionaries who apparently understood both the Christ-event and Christian life in "divine man" terms. They charged Paul with being a sham apostle who functioned in a purely human way (2 Corinthians 10:2) rather than by the power of the Spirit, as they themselves did. They claimed to be "of Christ" (2 Corinthians 10:2-4; 13:3). Corresponding to their view of Christ, the new Corinthian "apostles" (apostle does not refer to the Twelve but is used here in the inclusive sense, meaning something like "specially commissioned missionaries") understood the Christian life not as one of humble service but as egoistic assertiveness in the power of the Spirit (2 Corinthians 11:20, even allowing for Paul's irony). They naturally considered Paul's version of the Christian faith to be defective, lacking in the power that properly belonged to the Christian life, and they set out to remedy this defect in the Pauline churches. The Corinthian church responded positively to them, and when Paul visited Corinth to try to correct the situation, he was terribly humiliated and retreated, leaving the views of the new apostles to continue to dominate the church. Paul considers them false apostles, servants of Satan, disguising themselves as "superlative" apostles of Christ (2 Corinthians 11:5, 13-15).

These invectives are not simply the result of Paul's personal jealousy or small-minded inability to accept a differing theology as also a valid witness to the Christian faith. Paul's relation to Peter and Apollos and to their theologies, both of which were at variance with his own, and his commending them and their thought to the Corinthians, is itself a sufficient refutation of such a suggestion (1 Corinthians 3:1-23, especially vs. 21-22). Paul accepts—even celebrates—that there can be different theological expressions of the one Christian gospel. But more than that is at stake here.

74

Paul saw the "divine man" way of conceiving the Christ-event, and the resulting style of the Christian life which it fostered, as a fundamental perversion of the gospel rather than simply a different expression of it. And Paul's opponents regarded him in the same light. At Corinth, epiphany Christology, centered in a miracle-working Christ and miracle-working Christians (*theologia gloriae*), and kenosis Christology, centered in the crucified Christ and taking up one's cross as the mark of the Christian life (*theologia crucis*), violently confronted each other. Neither saw a way of accepting the other without surrendering itself.

We need first to see that there are two ways of doing theology, two theologies, which stand over against each other here. The argument was not a historical one, about what the "life of Jesus" was "really like," even if the proponents of each theology sometimes conducted the argument as though that were the case. Both theologies were ways of trying to express the "act of God" in Jesus. All such theological thinking must be in human thought-forms; all theology is human thinking about the divine. Even though Christian theology claims to be based on revelation, no one claims that the theology itself is revealed from heaven (the only exception being fundamentalism, which would make this claim for the theology in the Bible but not elsewhere). Thus every way of thinking about God's act, even in response to God's act in Jesus, is a product of finite human thinking, and therefore has both strengths and weaknesses.

Although it was apparently difficult for Paul to see them, there are some evident strengths of the epiphany Christology:

(1) It functions by describing events set within the earthly life of Jesus, filling in his human career with vivid pictures of salvation rather than relegating these to a cosmic drama beyond Jesus' earthly life.

(2) It pictures the threats to "life" from which we are saved by the Christ-event (hunger, sickness, guilt, loneliness, meaninglessness, death) as concrete realities within our everyday life pictorially and anecdotally, rather than as a list of abstractions or as mythological cosmic powers, thereby bringing the language of both salvation and damnation "down to earth." The stories, at least in their "human problem" dimension, are in continuity with the world in which we ordinarily live.

(3) The miracle stories expressing the epiphany Christology are also in continuity with the charismatic phenomena which actually characterized the life of the historical Jesus.

(4) The epiphany Christology makes the power of God in the Jesus-event dramatically *evident*. It is simply there in the story to be beheld, without any dialectical reflection. That is, it has all the values of a good story.

But the weaknesses of the epiphany Christology are also obvious:

(1) It pictures Jesus as a superman, a non-man. There is no place in it for a real death of Jesus, so that the crucifixion becomes a sham at the point where we are most human and most in need of God's presence. Since there is no real death of Jesus, there is no real resurrection either. The result is that Jesus' "resurrection" is understood as only another of Jesus' own mighty acts like those he performed during his ministry, by which instead of *dying* he passes triumphantly through crucifixion and burial by his own

mighty power. (Remember the active verbs in the Markan resurrection predictions.) Nor does the epiphany Christology have room for a real birth and childhood, which involves weakness, ignorance, vulnerability.

(2) Such a pattern for conceptualizing the work of God in the world teaches us to look for God's act only in the *extra*ordinary, in the *super*-human, thus at best removing large areas of our lives from becoming the vehicle of God's presence and power, at worst making us into curiosity-titillating miracle-mongers.

(3) Discipleship to such a Christ encourages us to think of the Christian life in triumphalistic terms, calls upon us to be supermen, identifying the Christian dimension of our own lives only with the *super*natural. (Cf. Paul's use of *super* terminology in 2 Corinthians 10—13 ironically opposing precisely this.)[22] This Christology contrasts Christ and humanity and so calls on us to be nonhuman in order to be Christians.

The weaknesses of the epiphany Christology are the strengths of the kenotic Christology, and vice versa. The values of kenotic Christology as a way of conceptualizing the Christ-event are seen in that:

(1) It is able to portray Jesus as living a life like our own, devoid of divine power, a life which fully shares our vulnerability and weakness, a life which ends in dying a real death. An almighty Jesus has no need of others, can have no friends. Aristotle's urbane observation is true to life:

> Friendship occurs where love is offered in return. But in friendship with God there is no room for love to be offered in return, indeed there is not even room for love. For it would be absurd if anyone were to assert that he loved Zeus.[23]

Only the weak God can be loved.

(2) Such a view of the act of God in Christ points us to the ordinary, the everyday, as the arena of God's act, and thus makes all our experience capable of mediating the divine presence and grace.

(3) Discipleship to such a Christ means identification with his cross, not with his triumphalistic power. Only such a view of the life of Jesus can transform our very weakness into an act of discipleship which may mediate the grace of God to others. Only such a view of God's act in Christ identifies our humanity as such as the *locus* of our following Christ, equating our human service to others with the service of God. The divine is no longer restricted to the strange and sensational.

But the weaknesses of kenosis Christology are also apparent. Suppose that Paul had so devastated his opponents at Corinth that epiphany Christology in any form had been banished from authentic Christian theology; i.e. suppose our New Testament contained only Paul's letters and the literature written on the Pauline model, such as Hebrews.

(1) We would hardly have any picture at all of the life of Jesus on this earth. We would know only "that" he had lived, that he had been a humble servant obedient to God, that he had suffered and died. According to Sören Kierkegaard: "If the contemporary generation had left nothing behind them but these words: 'We have believed that in such and such a year the God appeared among us in the humble figure of a servant, that he lived and

taught in our community, and finally died,' it would be more than enough."[24]

What is "enough" in this regard is a moot question, but there can be no doubt that Christian faith and life would be immeasurably the poorer without the stories of the Gospels picturing the nature of Jesus' life, just as there is no doubt that if the church had maintained an exclusively kenotic Christology, there would have been no reason to have preserved such stories. One need note, for instance, how blank the picture of Jesus' earthly life is in the Apostles' Creed. The central Act, the life of Jesus, is all but overwhelmed by the scenes of pre-existence and exaltation with which it is bracketed, so that the Jesus-story threatens to become a cosmic drama in which the earthly Jesus plays only a bit part.

(2) Likewise, in kenosis Christology the threats to human existence from which I am delivered are cosmic threats. In this scheme the everyday threats in which they are embodied do not become real to me, but it is the cosmic threat in *this* form with which I am actually faced. That "Death" as a cosmic power is overcome by the cosmic act of God in Christ is, no doubt, truly gospel, but I always concretely face the cosmic power of Death in some particular instance of dying. Kenosis Christology has no way to picture the concrete involvement of Jesus—and God—in Jairus' loss and gain. "Tis not Death but dying we fear" was always wrong, but Death cannot be abstracted from dying and still be real to me. Kenosis Christology has so magnified the dimensions of lostness that it is difficult for me to recognize them in the particulars of my finite existence.

(3) Kenosis Christology in fact denies something about the historical reality of Jesus' life, namely, that so far as we can tell it was characterized by healings and exorcisms. A Christology which must deny a part of the historical reality it attempts to interpret would seem to be sacrificing some facts to a theory. No doubt, Paul and his followers would dispute that these *were* facts, for he seems not to have believed that Jesus' life contained miraculous manifestations of the divine power, but we must judge otherwise and cannot accept a Christology as exclusively valid which does not make a place for the "facts" of Jesus' life.

(4) Kenosis Christology has no place for telling "stories about Jesus" as a vehicle of communicating the gospel. One can hardly imagine Paul in his Hellenistic churches telling stories about Jesus' exploits in Galilee. And yet the story form is irreplaceable; it can never become a disposable capsule from which its abstract "point" can be separated.

Mark Affirms Both Christologies

Prior to Mark there was no such thing as "Gospel" as a literary form, no narrative form which connected the individual incidents in the ministry of Jesus into a story which also included the death and resurrection. There were only individual units and clusters of tradition, some conceiving the life of Jesus in "divine man" terms, some in "kenosis" terms. The epiphany stories had no place for the cross; the kerygma of the cross and resurrection had no reason to tell miracle stories.

No doubt these were often held together in an unreflective way by the same person or congregation, just as they are today. This is testimony to the fact that none of the tradition was preserved for biographical purposes but that each item in the tradition was preserved because it bore its own witness to the meaning of the Christian faith. Many early Christians perceived this intuitively, and affirmed both types of the tradition about Jesus without even asking how they could be held together. This is still the case. Multitudes of committed church members, when reading the miracle stories in the Gospels, accept the superhuman picture of Jesus there given as representing how he actually was and then, later in the same Gospel, accept the Gethsemane and crucifixion account and are moved by it, without even asking how it can be that both are true. If the question does arise, it is usually resolved by one picture being sacrificed to the other, but for the most part it simply does not arise. So well has Mark done his work for us.

We have seen that in the pre-Markan church, when the difference in these two Christologies was perceived and reflected upon, they struggled with each other. Each way of seeing the Christ-event excluded the other, and was consistent in doing so. But we have also seen that each needed the other, that each had limitations which were supplemented by the strengths of the other. However, logic seems to dictate that there is no way of having it both ways without talking nonsense.

Back to the crucifixion scene in Mark: The logic of the chief priests certainly dictated that one must choose: either he is the Son of God and can come down from the cross, or he is not the Son of God and cannot. But Mark wants us to ask whether the chief priests' *way* of thinking is the last word on the matter. For there is another figure in the scene who gives an alternative response to the crucified Jesus. The centurion, a man without religious presuppositions or vocation, a man involved in the dirty work of the world where one's job sometimes calls for destruction of the innocent in order that the guilty be kept from destroying us all, a man who has seen no miracle and heard no sermon, save for the despairing cries of the dying figure before him, says *"Truly this man was the Son of God"* (15:39).

Just as Mark intends the chief priests' response to be the utterly wrong response of unbelief, he places the response which he considers the true response of faith in the mouth of the centurion. It is, in a sense, the punch line of the whole Gospel narrative, the thesis which Mark has ingeniously withheld until this final scene, but which now meets us as Mark's own faith. The confession made by the centurion, "Son of God," is the same confession found in the first line of Mark's Gospel as Mark's own declaration of the significance of Jesus. In 1:11 and 9:7, God himself acknowledges Jesus' identity as his own Son. The demons, with supernatural insight, recognize him as Son of God (3:11; 5:7). And Jesus himself claims this title in the encounter with the chief priest (14:62). But the only human being in the whole Gospel to whom the true identity of Jesus is disclosed is the centurion, who sees only the crucified one before him.

His terse affirmation has all that Mark wants to say. The confession declares that Jesus is "man" *(anthropos),* and not only that he is "a" man

78

but "this" man: precisely the one before him, in whom human weakness and victimization is concentrated. The confession declares that Jesus is "Son of God," that is, that he is "divine." And the confession prefixes to both of them the adverb "truly"; neither the manhood nor the divinity is compromised or diluted. Here is Mark's own confession of faith, in which the affirmation of both traditional Christologies finds expression.

For Mark affirms both ways of confessing faith in Jesus. We have seen that Mark himself takes up the "divine man" tradition in his Gospel in order to affirm it as a valid means of proclaiming the significance of the Christ-event (above, pp. 19-37). Mark does not introduce the extensive series of miracle stories and other testimony to the divinity of Jesus merely as a foil for the Christology which he really believes in, the theology of the cross. The "divine man" is not a straw man. But Mark also affirms the kenosis Christology, which he includes just as intentionally as the other (above, pp.15-54). Mark has both Christologies. He lets each picture of Jesus stand side by side without either diluting the other. He does not make Jesus into a composite figure, somewhat human but also somewhat divine, nor does he attempt a "synthesis" of the antithetical Christological traditions which had come to him in the tradition and which struggled against each other in his own church. Juxtaposition, not synthesis, is Mark's theological method. "Truly this *man* was the *Son of God.*"

The tension was too much for both Matthew and Luke. Luke changes the "divine" part so that "Son of God" becomes "righteous man" (Luke 23:47; some translations say "innocent"). Matthew changes the human part by prefixing the supernatural phenomena which (and not the crucified Jesus) became the basis for the centurion to declare Jesus to be the Son of God (Matthew 27:54).

Mark's method of juxtaposing the conflicting Christologies can be seen in the overall outline of which Mark himself is the author. Mark could have arranged the individual units of tradition that came to him in the tradition any way he pleased. He could, for instance, have alternated epiphany-Christology material with kenosis-Christology material throughout the Gospel, using first a miracle story, then a Gethsemane-like scene, then another miracle story, then another scene exhibiting Jesus' humanity and weakness. We have seen that there is some interweaving of the traits of human weakness with those of divine power in the Markan picture of Jesus.

But we may not have noticed that, unlike the other Gospels, Mark has gathered practically all the miracle material into the first half of the story. The other Gospels extend the miracle-working activity of Jesus right into the Passion story. But Mark places almost all the miracle material into the first half of the story, between the heavenly voice in 1:1 which declares him to be Son of God, and the reaffirmation of Jesus' divine Sonship in 9:7 by the same heavenly voice in the same words. Bracketed by these two heavenly declarations that Jesus is "truly Son of God," the miracle stories illustrate the meaning of this—from the perspective of the epiphany Christology. The few miracles that occur after 9:7 have another purpose in Mark's narrative than illuminating the saving meaning of the Christ-event in epiphany-Christology terms. The material which expresses the kenosis Christology, on the other hand, occurs mostly after the transfiguration scene. In rough outline, then, Mark's Gospel falls into two halves: "divine man" interpretation of Son of God, 1:1—9:7; and "kenosis" interpretation of Son of God, 9:8—16:8. These two are almost exactly the same in length, which suggests that the division is not arbitrary or a scholar's illusion, but corresponds to Mark's own outline. Schematically, then, Mark's Gospel appears to be two contrary pictures of Jesus juxtaposed to each other:

1:1	9:7	16:8
"power"		"weakness"
"divine man"		the human Jesus
Epiphany-Christology		Kenosis-Christology

This arrangement, then, in which Jesus is *both* "divine man" and "weak human" is an A.D. 70 reality of Mark's literary construction, not an attempt to portray the A.D. 30 reality of the "person" of Jesus. This point will be elaborated in chapter four.

This juxtaposition of two Christologies which characterized Mark as a whole is also manifest in several individual texts composed or edited by Mark:

Mark 1:1

Although the reader is not aware of it until he is well into the Gospel, in retrospect it seems clear that Mark's thesis is contained in the opening line of the text, which is probably intended as something of a title for the whole. The Gospel concerns Jesus Christ, the Son of God. Just as "Son of God" represents the divine reality manifest in Jesus, the name "Jesus" is a human name, the crucified man of Nazareth. The jolt has been dulled by repetition, but two worlds collide in this phrase, and Mark wants to affirm both of them.

Mark 1:2-3

The one who is addressed "offstage" in the "introit" with which the drama begins, the one who stands in the place of the Old Testament *kurios* (Lord), the one who is addressed by God the Father in a conversation which takes place somewhere beyond this world, the one who does what God himself was to do in the Old Testament text, *this* Divine One is also the one who has a "way" in this world that is prepared, a way which goes to the cross.

Mark 1:11

Jesus is addressed as both the divine Son of God *and* the servant of the Lord whose power is in his weakness, (see above, pp. 14, 50-51).

Mark 4:38-39

The one who is tired and asleep in the boat, in the care of the universe and the fishermen, is the one who calms the storm; the universe is in his care.

Mark 6:14-16

This is a curious passage. It is a scene which follows many miracles, but, although Herod and the others believe the miracles have happened, they do not conclude on this basis that he is the divine Son of God. Rather, he is considered to be John the Baptist who has been raised, or Elijah (who never died) who has come back from the heavenly world, or one of the old prophets who has come back from the dead. That is, he is seen as *more* than an ordinary man, but *less* than "truly divine." He is, in effect, semi-human, semi-divine. Thus Mark already contains, and repudiates, a *mistaken* way to come to terms with the "divine" and "human" ways of seeing Jesus, by placing these mistaken ideas in the mouths of Herod and the misbelieving populace.

Mark 6:49

In a pericope which has both human (Jesus prays, v. 46) and divine (walking on the water) characteristics, a second wrong way of handling these conflicting pictures of Jesus is pointed out by Mark: "They thought it was a ghost."

Mark 8:31; 9:31; 10:33; (9:9, 12)

In these "Passion predictions," carefully composed and structured by Mark himself from previous traditions, we again have the whole Gospel in miniature. Jesus is "truly human" in that he will suffer, be rejected, and be killed, the passive verbs testifying that he is weak-like-us. But he is also "truly divine" as the transcendent heavenly figure, the "Son of Man," whose path through suffering is not meaningless chance but moves according to the divine necessity *(dei)*. And after he is killed, he will rise (active verb) from the dead. Untypical of New Testament affirmations of the resurrection, Mark's active agent in the resurrection is not God who raises up Jesus but the (divine) Son of Man who raises himself. This bespeaks the powerful, not-like-us divine being in the face of death. At death, we are victims. But in each of these single sentences, Jesus is both victim and victor, both passive and powerful. Just as the Gospel as a whole was created by juxtaposing two Christologies, here we have a mini-Gospel, the divine and human affirmations about Jesus compressed into one sentence. Mark himself makes this identification in 8:32, Jesus preaches "the Word" *(logos=euanggelion,* "the gospel") to them.

Again, the tension is too much for Matthew and Luke. Both make the saying "consistent" (logically and theologically, not just grammatically) by changing *anastenai,* "rise again" (active), to *egerthenai,* "be raised" (passive).

Mark 10:45

As in 1:1 and 15:39, so also here, in one sharp juxtaposition of phrases the whole paradox is summed up. The Son of Man (the transcendent divine being who appears at the end of history with power over all the universe) will give his life (which only one who truly dies is able to do), and this as the supreme instance of his service for many. That the Son of Man should *serve* (not to speak of dying) was itself a mind-wrenching impossibility.

Mark 12:6-8

In the somewhat allegorized form in which the parable appears in Mark, the "beloved son" is both like and unlike the series of "servants" who are sent. [25] On the one hand, he is in the same series of commissionings from the owner as they, and like them he is weak, victimized, killed. On the other hand, he is Son, not slave, and is different from all the rest, standing uniquely (cf. the meaning of *agapetos,* "beloved," "only") on the same side as the Father.

Mark 14:61-62

"Are *you* the Christ, the son of the Blessed?" The pronoun is very emphatic in Mark's Greek text. Its presence in the sentence at all is emphatic, since it is not necessary and is usually absent in such Greek constructions. This emphasis is further strengthened by placing it first, so that it is not too strong to translate "Is it indeed *you* (the one who is in our power, the weak, about-to-be-crucified one, the one betrayed, denied, and abandoned) who is the Christ, the Son of God?" Jesus responds with an unequivocal "Yes" and then strengthens and interprets the "divine" side of the confession: He is the Son of Man who will be seated at the right hand of God, and who will be coming on the eschatological Day with the clouds of heaven. Mark could hardly make this point any clearer. Not only does he himself sum up the paradox in the first line of his Gospel (1:1) and place it in intensely concentrated form in the lips of the centurion at the climax of the crucial scene (15:39) but, in the one and only scene in the Gospel in which Jesus unambiguously discloses his own identity, he is the humiliated, crucified one at the mercy of his fellows who is also the mighty Son of God.

Mark 16:6

Almost as an epilogue, inside the tomb after the worst has happened (but an empty tomb that points to the act of *God:* "He *has been raised,"* passive), Jesus is spoken of in the most human terms. Surrounded by the framework of the act of God, the affirmation concerns only the crucified one.

Mark has it both ways. Both in the overall structure of his Gospel and in numerous individual texts he has held together the two pictures of Jesus, "inconfusedly, unchangeably, indivisibly, inseparably," as the later Chalcedonian creed said. *How* can Mark have it both ways? Must he not finally choose which of the pictures of Jesus he believes is the "real" one? Or even if, like the later Christian creeds, Mark believes that Jesus was "truly divine/truly human," how can he do justice to both pictures of Jesus in the same narrative?

We must remember that Mark was the first to attempt to do this. There was as yet no Gospel which he could adapt as a model. Mark himself devised the literary form of the Gospel in order to affirm both the "divine man" Christology with its emphasis on miracles and the "kenosis"

Christology's concentration on the cross. In the first of these, Jesus' messianic power was obvious during his ministry. In the second, he was seen to be the Christ by faith only after the crucifixion and resurrection. To gain some insight into what Mark has done for us here, we need to look closely at this development of the "messianic secret" motif in the construction of this narrative.

Messianic Secret, Gospel Form, and Christological Language

Since we unfortunately tend to allow the pictures of Jesus in the four Gospels to merge with each other in a way that blurs the distinctive presentation of each author, we may not have noticed the rather peculiar way in which Mark constructs his narrative. The characters in the story do not discern Jesus' true identity until the story is over. The disciples misunderstand him, even his relatives fail to perceive, and Jesus himself does not disclose his identity until the final scene (14:61-62). This is in contrast, for example, to the Gospel of John, where Jesus is recognized immediately as the Christ, the Son of God, the Son of Man, etc., publicly discusses his claim to be Son of God (John 1:29-51; 5:10-29), and denies that he has taught anything secretly (John 18:20). This cluster of materials scattered throughout Mark, which suggests that during his ministry Jesus was not recognized and understood by the participants in the story as the Christ or Son of God, or that, if recognized, it was to be kept secret until the resurrection, is called the "messianic secret."[26]

To get the picture of how Mark has composed his story, we need first to comb through Mark and notice all the texts in which he pictures Jesus as being less than public about his true identity. The reader will need to follow the text of Mark and note the following data:

1:1. From the first line onwards, the *reader* knows who Jesus really is. He knows something the participants in the story do not know. Thus the messianic secret is *not* the kind of literary device which preserves the mystery from the reader (as in a detective story of the whodunit variety), saving the disclosure of Jesus' real identity for the last climactic scene. It is rather a device for explaining why the characters in the pre-Easter story did not recognize Jesus for what he really was, and it presupposes that this recognition came only after the resurrection.

1:10. Only Jesus sees the heavens opened.

1:11. The address of the heavenly voice is only to Jesus. The *reader* "overhears" the declaration from heaven that Jesus is the divine Son, but no one in the story does. (Contrast Matthew's rewriting of this, Matthew 3:17. Matthew has his own way of telling the story, which does not include the messianic secret.)

1:24. The demons, by supernatural knowledge, know who Jesus is, so he commands silence. Too late! They have already disclosed the secret. But in 1:27 this disclosure seems to have had no effect at all. The crowd is still ignorant of Jesus' true identity and asks, "What is this?" This tension in the narrative is our first hint that the secrecy motif may be a later overlay on the original story. So again, the disclosure is to the *reader,* not the persons in the story.

1:34. Jesus would not permit the demons to speak, because they knew him.

1:44. After healing the leper, Jesus insists that he tell no one. This has often been explained in terms of the A.D. 30 history of Jesus, the reason for such commands to silence supposedly being that, if word of such healings became too widespread, Jesus would be mobbed with requests for healing and would be unable to continue his ministry or would prematurely provoke a confrontation with the authorities. If the Gospel of Mark is taken as a transcript of the life of Jesus, then some such psychological explanation (which is found nowhere in the text) must be supplied in order to make sense of the story.

But we have repeatedly seen that Mark is doing something with his materials besides writing straight biography. The purported biographical explanation, here and elsewhere, is not as helpful as it appears at first. If Jesus exercised the supernatural power to heal leprosy, then why should he be bothered by the possibility of being "overwhelmed by the crowds"? Surely his supernatural power could handle that too. And it is a curious kind of healing which restores physical wholeness but denies to the healed man the reunion with the world of his loved ones, the separation from whom must have been as painful as the disease itself. So, one begins to see that the messianic secret does not function at the level of explaining the biographical events of the A.D. 30 life of Jesus but has its meaning at some other level.

2:12. After claiming to have the divine power to forgive sins, and "proving" it by his healing the paralyzed man, the crowds, still in ignorant mystification, do not identify Jesus.

3:7-10. In 2:1—3:6, Mark takes over and reworks a cluster of materials which had apparently already congealed to some extent in the pre-Markan tradition.[27] In this cluster of traditions, Jesus functioned publicly (compare the literal reading of 3:3 "stand forth in the midst," with Mark's own view) with an authority which he himself claimed to be divine. Mark edits this cluster of traditions himself, imposing his own editorial patterns upon it, but the publicity motif of 2:10; 2:28; and 3:3 were in the pre-Markan tradition. When Mark himself begins to compose freely again in 3:7, he has Jesus withdraw from the publicity given him in 2:1—3:6, and in 3:10 his characteristic command to silence reappears.

3:21, 31-35. Jesus' identity is concealed even from his family members, who think he is crazy. In Mark, they never penetrate his secret. This is the only picture Mark gives us of Mary and Jesus' brothers and sisters: standing "outside" with those who do not understand (cf. 4:11!).

4:10-12. In Mark, the parables are not understood by the multitude, and are not even intended by Jesus to be understood by them. Jesus privately explains the parables to his disciples, but they serve to conceal the truth from the crowds. This description of a teacher who himself conceals what he is teaching from his hearers seemed so strange to Matthew that he again rewrote it to place the responsibility for the crowds' lack of understanding on their own dullness, not on the intention of Jesus (Matthew 13:10-17). Although this is psychologically more understandable and certainly fits more readily into our reconstruction of what the A.D. 30 ministry of Jesus must have been like (so that we typically follow Matthew at this point and Mark's strange view of Jesus' parables has scarcely been noticed), we are again challenged by the text to ask whether Mark is at all interested in composing a biographical account of what it was "really like" in the A.D. 30 ministry of Jesus.

4:22. A traditional saying is used by Mark to assert that though (in the story) the secret is to be kept now, there will come a time when it will be revealed to all. Mark does not here indicate when that time will be, but does give the reader the clue that the messianic secret is only temporary. The true identity of Jesus and the meaning of his message *will* be disclosed, but not yet.

4:34. Mark's closing summary of the day spent in teaching in parables reinforces the view he had given in 4:10-12 discussed above. The reader should not misunderstand: Jesus' public teaching was not understood during his ministry and was not intended to be. It was only to his disciples that the understanding was given.

4:41. But even the "understanding" of his disciples is called in question in the very next scene. They, unlike the crowds, had had the opportunity to perceive Jesus' message and identity. But they clearly had not done so. Even though Jesus displays his power over the demon-storm, the disciples can only rub their eyes and ask, "Who is this?"

5:7. The demons continue to recognize him and to announce his identity. This continues to have no effect on the people in the story.

5:19. Jesus had healed the man of his demon possession. Then the man is told to go and proclaim what "the Lord" had done for him. The reader knows that Jesus is the Lord. But the title "Lord" is ambiguous to the people in the story, who take it to refer to God, who is commonly called "Lord" in the Old Testament and in the synagogue worship. A similar ambiguity applies to the term "Lord" in each of the few places it is used with reference to Jesus throughout the Gospel of Mark. It is either used in the vocative case in such a way that it can also be taken as the polite form of address (as 7:28, cf. Matthew 27:63, where the same word used in addressing Pilate is translated "Sir"), or used with intentional ambiguity as in 11:3, where the Greek can be understood either as "The Lord has need of it" or "Its master needs it." Luke and John do not hesitate to publicly disclose Jesus as "Lord" during his ministry (Luke 7:13, 19; 10:1; John 4:1; 6:23; 11:2). Mark never allows Jesus to be called "Lord" in the Christological sense but uses this term with an ambiguity which is almost cunning.

5:43. After Jesus has brought the funeral to an end and dramatically presented the girl alive and instructed her to be fed, there follows the command that no one is to know about this! Here the incongruity of this as an actual event in the A.D. 30 life of Jesus is most clear. Again, the messianic secret motif seems to be a later overlay, not part of the original story, and it seems to serve a different function from the story itself.

6:2-3. The hometown folk acknowledge Jesus' mighty works but do not penetrate the secret of his person, and in the end they chase him out.

6:31f. Again, this is a typical scene of Jesus shunning publicity, wanting to be alone with his disciples.

6:48-52. Though Jesus walks on the sea, the disciples respond in awe and terror. In v. 52, they do not understand because of the (divine?) hardening of their hearts. Mark suggests not only that they did not understand but that they *could* not understand. Something is yet lacking before understanding of who Jesus is can occur. There have been only hints thus far as to what this may be (2:20; 3:6). Once again, Matthew finds this impossible, and has the disciples praise Jesus as the Son of God (Matthew 14:33).

7:17ff. As in 4:10-12 and 4:34, Jesus' teaching is explained only in private, and its meaning is withheld from the crowds.

7:31-37. Jesus performs the miracle privately, and when it is completed commands silence—to a man to whom he has just given the gift of speech! Something besides A.D. 30 biography is going on here. The concluding line is what we have come to expect by now: They are impressed but do not know who Jesus is.

8:17-21. The disciples, supposedly initiated into the secret of Jesus' teaching about the kingdom of God, and having seen both the miraculous feedings, here have the same words applied to them as are applied to the "outsiders" in 4:11-12. This is especially significant in view of the fact that this section must certainly be the free composition of Mark himself. The feedings of the 5000 and of the 4000 were variations of the same story. Mark included them both, and this incident in the boat refers to both, so it must be entirely editorial. It is Mark, not the tradition, who is emphasizing that not even the disciples understood who Jesus was or the significance of his mighty acts during his ministry.

8:26. As usual, the healing of the blind man is to be kept secret.

8:27-30. In the context of several wrong answers concerning Jesus' identity, Peter gives the "right answer." Jesus *is* the Christ as Mark had already told the reader (1:1). But it turns out that Jesus' response to Peter's "confession" is ambiguous in the extreme, neither accepting it nor rejecting it, and that in any case the disciples are commanded not to say that Jesus is the Christ to anyone else.

9:2-10. The transfiguration is a secret epiphany of Christ's glory. Three chosen disciples see it and hear the heavenly voice which acknowledges Jesus to be the divine Son. It is not clear that they understand the significance of what they have seen, but in any case they are commanded to be quiet about it *until the resurrection.* This is the first time that the *terminus* of the secret is disclosed. This disclosure had to wait until Jesus had announced his coming suffering and death (8:31), and this announcement had to wait until he was confessed as the Christ. At this point the reader sees for the first time that the messianic secret is to be dissolved at, and by, the crucifixion-resurrection event. At *that* point, and not before, Jesus will be disclosed for what he really is, which has already been disclosed to the (post-resurrection) reader.

9:28-32. This is the last clear reference to the messianic secret, though there are a few other references to the private nature of Jesus' teachings, e.g.

13:4. But these no longer concern the secrecy of the messiahship. Except for the healing of Bartimaeus in 10:46-52, this is the last of Jesus' healings. Except for the withering of the fig tree in 11:12ff., there are no more miracles in Mark. Thus from 9:33 on, there is very little reference to the messianic secret, though Mark assumes that it is kept. The messianic secret is prominent in the same section of the Gospel which has the epiphany Christology, and only there. (Recall the structure of the Gospel as a whole which Mark has created, discussed on pp. 77-80.) From this point on, the *meaning* of the messiahship, rather than the secret fact of it, is Mark's concern.[28] Thus the references to the messianic secret in 9:28, 30, 32 come as a kind of final statement of it, in conjunction with the prediction of the cross-resurrection event.

How should we understand this mass of material in Mark which expresses the "messianic secret"? Basically two answers have been given to this question: (1) that the secret messiahship more or less accurately represents the actual nature of Jesus' ministry, and (2) that the messianic secret is the post-Easter creation of the church.

The typical explanation of those who believe the messianic secret to be historical is that, although Jesus did in fact believe that he was the Messiah, he understood messiahship in radically different terms from his contemporaries. If he had allowed his messiahship to be known, he would have been inevitably misunderstood. So, although he worked messianic miracles and privately acknowledged that he was the Messiah, he forbade it to be publicized until the proper time. In this view, the messianic secret is a tactic of the historical Jesus.

The second view, that the messianic secret was the creation of Mark himself, has far more evidence in its favor, and is accepted by the great majority of critical scholars for the following reasons:

(1) In all our New Testament documents, the idea of the secret messiahship is found only in Mark and in documents dependent on Mark. The earliest collection of Jesus-materials which we can isolate, the Q source, which is considerably older than Mark, contains neither claims by Jesus to be the Christ, nor commands to keep his identity or mighty works a secret. The contrary, in fact, is the case (cf., e.g., Matthew 11:2-6/Luke 7:18-23). Matthew and Luke have the "messianic secret" idea only in those passages that they have incorporated from Mark or that have been influenced by him (and, as we have seen, not in all of these, since both Matthew and Luke adapt some of them to their own view of the public messiahship of Jesus during his ministry). The materials peculiar to Matthew ("M") and to Luke ("L") do not contain the messianic secret motif, nor do the editorial additions of either evangelist. In the Gospel of John, Jesus is publicly understood to be the Messiah, the Son of God, etc. (or claiming to be such) from the first chapter onwards (1:29-30, 45, 49, 51; 4:26; 6:69; 8:42, 58; 9:37; 10:36; etc.) and explicitly repudiates the idea that his true teaching was essentially private (John 18:20).

(2) In Mark, the secrecy material is primarily in the editorializing, not in the traditional materials themselves.[29] We have noted several places where it appears that there was an original story in which some mighty deed made

Jesus' messianic dignity obvious. Then, in a second editorial layer incongruously laid over the original story, the command was given not to tell of the miracle coupled with a kind of blind nonrecognition of Jesus despite the miracle. (Cf. the discussion of 1:24; 2:12; 4:41; 5:43; pp. 83-85.)

(3) We have also noted the many places where the messianic secret motif is extremely difficult to imagine historically (e.g. 5:43). In several places Matthew and/or Luke, the first interpreters of Mark, changed the text in order to make a more believable, consistent story. Whatever the meaning of Mark's messianic secret, it does not seem to be that of accurately representing the A.D. 30 reality of Jesus' ministry.

(4) The evidence is that Jesus himself made no *explicitly* messianic claims, but that the messianic confessions in the Gospels represent the faith of the post-Easter church, which first made explicit the implicit messianism of Jesus' life in the full light of the cross and resurrection.

This evidence seems to be so compelling that most scholars consider the messianic secret to be essentially Mark's own creation, though based on embryonic beginnings in the earlier tradition, some of which may go back into the ministry of the historical Jesus. But why? Why burden the narrative with such an ungainly and difficult-to-imagine perspective? The first answer given to this question was from the scholar who first observed and analyzed the secrecy motif in Mark, William Wrede.[30]

Wrede's view was that Mark devised the messianic secret to explain the fact that the church confessed faith in Jesus as the messiah, although the actual life of Jesus had been entirely unmessianic. According to Wrede, Mark's response to this problem, which must have been a charge the church faced from outsiders, was: Jesus' life *had* been messianic, but it had been kept a secret until after the resurrection. Thus the messianic secret served the purpose of making the life of Jesus appear more messianic than it had in fact been. It functioned, so to speak, to up the Christological ante, to messianize an essentially unmessianic tradition about Jesus.

We owe Wrede a great deal for his initial discovery and analysis of the secrecy motif in Mark, but he appears to have been entirely wrong as to Mark's reason for creating the secrecy theme. His theory shatters on the fact that there never was an unmessianic version of the tradition about Jesus. The confession that Jesus was the messiah permeated the tradition from the beginning, and was the very reason it was handed down in the church. The current view of Mark's purpose is almost the exact opposite of Wrede's, and it is much more supportable: The traditions of the ministry of Jesus, especially the miracle stories, were already entirely *too* Christological in Mark's view, because they represented Jesus as Messiah quite apart from the cross-resurrection *kerygma* (preaching). But Mark was also committed to the Christology which held the cross-resurrection event to be indispensable. So Mark devised a literary method of holding the two together, allowing the "divine man" and "cross-resurrection" *kerygmas* to "correct" each other. This view is widely accepted today, and there is an aspect of it that I wish to develop more precisely.

As I see it, Mark's problem was that he had two basically different Christologies struggling with each other in his church. Although the proponents of each Christology seemed not to see the values of the other, Mark saw the value of both. But they had conflicting pictures of the way the earthly Jesus had appeared during his ministry. Mark developed the messianic secret as a literary device to enable him, within one narrative form, to contain both pictures, both Christologies. In Mark, as in the kenosis Christology, Jesus' true identity does not become manifest until the cross-resurrection, when Jesus truly dies as weak-like-us. But also, in Mark, the messianic power is already at work within Jesus' life, as in the epiphany Christology, where he is the "strong Son of God" not-like-us. The framework within which both these views are affirmed and held in tension is that of the messianic secret. In the narrative framework which the messianic secret makes possible, Jesus' messianic miracles can be portrayed, but they were not known or understood as such until after the resurrection, by Jesus' specific command. However historically incongruous this may seem does not matter to Mark, for he claimed not to be writing history but a Gospel. The Gospel is a new A.D. 70 reality, not an abortive effort to reproduce an A.D. 30 reality. This is the new literary genre *created* by Mark, a narrative framework in which the two opposing Christologies may be held together and affirmed in such a way that each would dialectically balance the other. This is what a Gospel *is*. "The secrecy theory is the hermeneutical presupposition of the genre 'gospel.'"[31]

To the extent that they preserve this tensive juxtaposition of pictures of the Jesus who is truly human and truly divine without compromising either side of the paradox, Matthew, Luke, and John also belong to the literary genre "Gospel." Matthew and Luke both use Mark as a major source for their own Gospels, and thus to a considerable extent simply elaborate and amplify the form created by Mark. Whether or not the author of the fourth Gospel knew Mark is a disputed point among New Testament scholars. In any case, John manifests the same combination of "truly human" and "truly divine" pictures of Jesus, whether he derived this from Gospels already in circulation or created it himself. In the latter case, he too is credited with the creation of the Gospel genre. However this may have been, Mark was the first Christian author to bring the two streams of Christology together in one narrative, and he did so by means of the messianic secret.

The messianic secret is not in itself an object of faith or theological method. It is the means to an end in that it makes possible a narrative structure within which a distinctive kind of language can be expressed. The Gospel-form, which the messianic secret makes possible, provides a narrative framework within which both pictures of Jesus, the "truly divine" and the "truly human," may be held together with equal force. Mark does not present us with a composite Jesus, partly-divine and partly-human. There is no harmonizing or synthesizing of the pictures. They remain two pictures. Jesus' humanity and divinity are not handled in terms of a single 50/50 picture, or even a 60/40 or 90/10. While the proponents of each of the Christologies were consistent in their picture of the life of Jesus, picturing it as either divine or human, Mark seems to have lost this consistency in attempting to have it both ways. His picture is of a 100/100 figure! "Truly divine"/"truly human" language seems to be a logically troublesome way of thinking and speaking which may even appear meaningless. But it is nonetheless a kind of language which Mark has intentionally developed, not fallen into, to say what must be said about the meaning of the Christ-event.

What *is* this kind of language?

For Further Reading

Brown, Raymond, *Jesus, God and Man*. Macmillan, 1967.

Burkill, T. A., *Mysterious Revelation: An Examination of the Philosophy of St. Mark's Gospel*. Cornell University Press, 1963.

Craddock, Fred B., *The Gospels*. Abingdon, 1981.

Kelber, Werner H., *Mark's Story of Jesus*. Fortress Press, 1979.

Kingsbury, Jack Dean, *The Christology of Mark's Gospel*. Fortress Press, 1983.

Martin, Ralph, *Mark: Evangelist and Theologian*. Zondervan, 1972.

Rhoads, David, and Michie, Donald, *Mark as Story: An Introduction to the Narrative of a Gospel*. Fortress Press, 1982.

Tucket, Christopher, *The Messianic Secret*. Fortress Press, 1983.

Wrede, William, *The Messianic Secret*. James Clark and Co., Ltd., 1971.

4

The Gospel as Language

Paradoxical Language

The kind of language found in the Gospel of Mark and elsewhere in the New Testament that spoke of Jesus as both truly human and truly divine was accepted in the church as the only authentic way of confessing faith in *God*'s act in *Jesus*. Inadequate and perverse ways of thinking and speaking about Jesus developed—heresies—with the result that a series of councils of theologians and church leaders was held to formulate authentic ways of articulating the Christian confession. Since the debate was carried on among trained philosophers who wanted the church's language to be able to hold its own in intellectual circles, the narrative and pictorial language of the Bible was replaced in their creeds and statements by the conceptually precise language of philosophical discussion.

After much controversy, the church adopted at Constantinople in 381 a formula which has come to be called "The Nicene Creed." It clearly affirmed that it is no other than the eternal God who is met in the man Jesus Christ:

I believe in one God the Father Almighty, Maker of heaven and earth, And of all things visible and invisible:

And in one Lord Jesus Christ, the only-begotten Son of God; Begotten of his Father before all worlds, God of Gods, Light of Light, Very God of Very God; Begotten, not made; Being of one substance with the Father; By whom all things were made: Who for us men and for our salvation came down from heaven, And was incarnate by the Holy Ghost of the Virgin Mary, And was made man: And was crucified also for us under Pontius Pilate; He suffered and was buried: And the third day he rose again according to the Scriptures: And ascended into heaven, And sitteth on the right hand of the Father: And he shall come again, with glory, to judge both the quick and the dead; Whose kingdom shall have no end.

And I believe in the Holy Ghost, The Lord, and Giver of Life, Who proceedeth from the Father and the Son; Who with the Father and the Son together is worshipped and glorified; Who spake by the Prophets: And I believe in one Catholic and Apostolic Church: I acknowledge one Baptism for the remission of sins: And I look for the Resurrection of the dead: And the Life of the world to come. Amen.[32]

For Catholic Christianity (i.e., the mainstream, orthodox church) this settled the issue of the legitimacy of language about Jesus Christ which affirmed him to be the incarnation of the one eternal God. Although the Nicene Creed also clearly affirmed that Christ was one who had become human and suffered, disputes continued for more than a hundred years concerning the proper way of thinking and speaking about the humanity of Jesus. The definitive statement was finally achieved at the Council of Chalcedon in A.D. 451:

We, then, following the holy Fathers, all with one consent, teach men to confess one and the same Son, our Lord Jesus Christ, the same perfect in Godhead and also perfect in manhood; truly God and truly man, of a reasonable soul and body; consubstantial with the Father according to the Godhead, and consubstantial with us according to the Manhood; in all things like unto us, without sin; begotten before all ages of the Father according to the Godhead, and in these latter days, for us and for our salvation, born of the Virgin Mary, the Mother of God, according to the Manhood; one and the same Christ, Son, Lord, Only-begotten, to be acknowledged in two natures, inconfusedly, unchangeably, indivisibly, inseparably; the distinction of natures being by no means taken away by the union, but rather the property of each nature being preserved, and concurring in one Person and one Subsistence, not parted or divided into two persons, but one and the same Son, and only-begotten, God the Word, the Lord Jesus Christ; as the prophets from the beginning have declared concerning him, and the Lord Jesus Christ himself has taught us, and the Creed of the holy Fathers has handed down to us.[33]

We are not concerned here with the ancient philosophical terminology in which this creed is expressed, language which to us may seem unnecessarily abstruse and abstract, but with the central pair of affirmations which the creed labors to express and safeguard: that "Jesus Christ our Lord" was "truly God and truly man." This kind of language is usually, and properly,

92

called "paradox" or "paradoxical language." But since the word "paradox" is used by logicians, scientists, philosophers, and in common parlance in a wide variety of senses, what I intend by the term in this discussion needs to be made more precise.

Surface Paradox and Depth Paradox

Paradoxos is a Greek word, the etymological meaning of which is "contrary to [the common] opinion." The word "paradox" does not occur in Mark, but in Luke's account of the healing of the paralytic, the crowd responds by saying "We have seen *strange things* [literally "paradoxes"] today" (Luke 5:25).

In general usage, paradox is any sort of language which is surprising to the mind. Such language goes against the grain of the way we normally think, bringing the mind up short. This general kind of paradox is not a violation of logic but a lively, startling way of expression which jogs the mind and gets beneath its surface in a way which ordinary communication does not.

"The difficult we do immediately; the impossible takes a little longer." This motto of the "Seabees" of World War II is a typical example of such language. It is a catchy way of saying something, the meaning of which is quite clear, and which can be said in a more straightforward, if less arresting manner: The Seabees specialize in jobs ordinarily considered difficult or impossible. Phillip Wheelwright calls such language "surface paradox."[34]

Surface paradoxes are a valuable form of communication. They are not superficial. Martin Luther began his essay on Christian freedom with this "paradoxical" assertion:

> A Christian is perfectly free Lord of all, subject to none. A Christian is perfectly dutiful servant of all, subject to all.[35]

When the mind meets such pairs of conflicting statements, if it takes them seriously and does not just regard them as nonsense, it instinctively attempts to resolve them into one comprehensive, nonparadoxical statement which does justice to both conflicting terms. One common way is to "distinguish the terms," that is, to understand that the key words are used differently in each statement, so that each sentence can be true in its own sense. Or another means of resolving such conflicting statements is to find the partial truth in each side of the paradox, and to combine these partial truths into one harmonious statement. This was the approach of Aristotle,[36] who did not simply reject conflicting pairs of statements but considered that each of them had been made with good reason, and searched for the partial truth in each which he then synthesized into one comprehensive statement containing the "whole" truth in nonconflicting terms.

The above examples are "paradoxical" language only in the general sense that they are unexpected and startling. Neither of them presents any fundamentally logical difficulties. But in designating the kind of Christological language of the New Testament and the classical Christian creeds as paradoxical language, I intend a very specific kind of language:

By paradoxical language I mean an irreducible pair of affirmations, in logical tension with each other in such a way that it seems that if one of them is true, the other cannot be. Henceforth, this is what I shall mean by the terms "paradoxical language," "paradox," or "Christological language." In contrast to the "surface paradox" discussed above, Wheelwright calls this "depth paradox," which aims "directly at some transcendent truth which is so mysterious and many-sided in its suggestions of meaningful possiblities that either half of the paradox taken alone would be grossly inadequate and partisan."[37] Such language is exemplified in the Gospels' pairing of statements about Jesus in which he is both "truly human" (weak-like-us) and "truly divine" (powerful-like-God), and in the declaration of the Chalcedonian creed that Jesus Christ our Lord is "truly God and truly man."

The logical difficulties in affirming such pairs of statements are clear. If Jesus were truly human and *also* truly divine, how could he be truly human, for an essential ingredient of true humanity is not being divine. The Markan Jesus either *was able* to come down from the cross as the "truly divine" being implied by the miracle stories, or he was *not* able to do so as a "truly human" being who shares our human weakness and death. These statements seem incapable of being logically affirmed together. To the logical mind, they appear to be either/or, not both/and statements.

The *form* of such language is important. Christological language has the form of two contrary statements affirmed in tandem. The two statements are irreducible. That is, they cannot be combined into some third statement which synthesizes and harmonizes them. In terms of formal logic, the pairs of statements are contraries, not contradictories.[38] If the Christological pair of statements were placed in contradictory form, two pairs of statements would be required: "Jesus is truly human/Jesus is not truly human" and "Jesus is truly divine/Jesus is not truly divine," with each pair of statements being a self-contradiction. If Christological language were self-contradictory, it would indeed be illegitimate. But the positive statements "Jesus is truly human/Jesus is truly divine," though they are logically troublesome as contraries, are not self-contradictory. We will deal with the relation of paradoxical language to strict logic in a later section, but we should note here that while in strict logic contraries cannot both be true, contraries are not self-contradictions, and Christological language should not be called contradictory.

Although the form of paradoxical language calls for two conflicting statements to be affirmed together, this form may be implicit in a single statement. The confession "Jesus is the Christ" is an example of "paradox" in the general sense. So understood, it is not a *logically* troublesome statement, only a culturally shocking one in first-century Judaism. But understood another way, the statement contains implicitly the basic Christological paradox in the more specific sense, in that it implicitly juxtaposes two statements which seem incapable of being affirmed together. As used in the New Testament and the early church, the common human name "Jesus" represents a claim to the true humanity of Jesus, the man of Nazareth. But in the New Testament, "Christ" is no longer the human deliverer of Israel by God's power but is used as a synonym for, and parallel to, "Son of God," "Son of Man," "Lord," and even "God," all titles claiming full divinity. To say that Jesus (the truly human one) is the Christ (the truly divine one) is equivalent to saying "Jesus is truly human/Jesus is truly divine." Understood in this way, the basic confession "Jesus is the Christ" is paradoxical language in the strict sense, although the form is only implicit.

Both "surface paradox" and "depth paradox" are found in the New Testament but Christological language, strictly speaking, is depth paradox. Depth paradoxes cannot be reduced to nonparadoxical language without violating them or losing them. They function to communicate the truth not by stimulating the mind to seek a statement which combines them and relaxes the tension, but precisely by maintaining the tension. Jesus was not "partly human" and "partly divine," nor was he "in a sense human" and "in a sense divine" in some way that these "senses" can be combined in one nonparadoxical statement which states what Jesus "really" was. In Christological language the paradox is ultimate.

The Variety of Kinds of Valid Language

Paradoxical language is a certain *kind* of language. Part of our difficulty in coming to terms with paradoxical language in the New Testament and Christian theology is our common assumption of the homogeneity of language. Yet a moment's reflection will reveal that all language is not of the same kind. The sentence "I do" is one kind of language in response to the question "Does anyone here know how to fly a helicopter?" and another kind of language in response to the question "Do you take this woman to be your lawful wedded wife?" It is not just that the meaning of the two-word sentence is changed by the shift in the context in which it is uttered. A fundamental linguistic shift occurs between the two situations. Two different *kinds* of language are represented here. The first "I do" is descriptive language; the second is performative language. The former instance functions to pass along information. Whether it is trivia or vital information in which the speaker is existentially involved, the language is informational, and its truth-function is judged in terms of whether the information it purports to deliver accords with empirical facts. It is a true and valid kind of language, without which we could not live as human beings. The same is true of the second "I do," although it is not informational at all. It functions by performing the action it names. It too has appropriate criteria by which its truth-function and validity can be ascertained, but these are not the same kind of criteria appropriate to informational language. Though composed of identical-looking "I do's," these two sentences represent two very different kinds of language, each of which is true and valid for its own function.

A generation ago, there flourished a kind of linguistic philosophy called logical positivism, which asserted that only empirical, scientific language is meaningful.[39] All language that is not subject to empirical verification was pronounced neither true nor false but meaningless. In the days of the post-

World War II technology race, when the big powers of both East and West idealized the scientist, the supposedly objective, realistic language of the laboratory was taken as the standard of all valid language. All language which could not be "verified" (at least in principle) in the same manner as the scientists' language was regarded as merely expressing the speaker's feelings, not referring to anything real. The "scientific" mood of the culture on which linguistic analysis fed in those days tended to make a whole generation of writers in philosophy, literature, and theology defensive or apologetic, feeling guilty that their language did not "measure up" to empirical standards.

But linguistic analysis turned out to be not the wave of the future but only a receding ripple on the surface of the history of philosophy. The motto of verification analysis, "the meaning of a sentence is the method of its verification," was replaced by the watchword of functional analysis, "the meaning of language is found in its use." Linguistic philosophy shifted from a *prescriptive* claim that there is only one kind of truth-functional language to the *descriptive* task of analyzing the ways in which language actually is used. This is where the focus of interest in linguistic philosophy is presently located.

From the point of view of our present discussion, the chief accomplishment of linguistic philosophy has been in establishing that there are several different types of language, or "language games," which differ from each other in kind. It was Ludwig Wittgenstein who taught us that there is no all-embracing language game that sets the rules for all language that would claim to be meaningful, but a number of different language games, each with its own rules. No language game may be judged by the rules appropriate to another game, nor may the games as such be ranked on a scale in terms of their capacity to express the truth. Each language game is related to reality, and mediates truth, in a way appropriate to itself.

Wittgenstein began his philosophical career advocating a position near the old logical positivism, arguing that the validity of language was its 1:1 correspondence with reality. Later, this same Ludwig Wittgenstein led the shift to the functional analysis of language. In one of his later writings he graphically pictured the variety of valid types of language within which we live:

> Our language can be seen as an ancient city: a maze of little streets and squares, of old and new houses, and of houses with additions from various periods; and this surrounded by a multitude of new boroughs with straight regular streets and uniform houses.[40]

Truth does not inhabit only one house, or one type of house, in the linguistic city, nor do we.

A few moments' reflection can readily identify several types of language, some of which are listed here for purposes of illustration, not as an exhaustive list. To illuminate the point, all the examples use the word "you."

1. *Analytical language*—"'You' is a three-letter word in the English language." The language functions to analyze what is already present in the language. "A triangle is a three-sided plane figure" is analytical language,

as are many definitions. "Two plus two is four" is analytical language, as is the language of mathematics in general. Such language functions to explicate what is already given, not to provide any new information. Analytical language deals with words, not facts; it is not geared into the world objective to the language itself. (Two quarts of milk plus two quarts of marbles do not make four quarts of anything.)

2. *Empirically descriptive language*—"You are less than six feet tall." This is the language of the laboratory and of much of our ordinary descriptive conversation. It functions to describe and measure, in ways that can be checked empirically. It refers to the objective world, and attempts to give information about it in such a way that the language corresponds as closely as possible to objective reality.

3. *Imperative language*—"You open the door." Imperative language functions to get something done by someone else. It may be imperative in form, as in the example above, but it may have other forms as well. "The doctor told me not to get too hot" or "Since the sun came out the temperature certainly has risen in this stuffy little room" may also be imperative language, and not necessarily the descriptive language they appear to be on the surface.

4. *Performative language*—"I forgive you." Performative language performs the action described. "He forgave her" is descriptive language, as is "I forgave you." But "I forgive you" is different in kind from either.

5. *Interrogative language*—"Do you forgive me?" It may function to obtain information, but is also used in other ways. It may be an expression of apology or repentance. It may challenge the questioned one, or be used to wound: "Do *you* (after what you have done, dare to) forgive *me*?" These examples have already shifted to another kind of language, although they remain interrogative in form, and partially in function.

6. *Expressive language*—"You light up my life." Expressive language functions to express the feelings of the speaker, sometimes with and sometimes without the intention of arousing feelings in the person addressed. It may or may not exhibit logical structure.

7. *Confessional language,* sometimes called *convictional language*—"I love you." This is the language of one who confesses his experience of something, or who is overcome, "convicted," by some external reality, so that he responds with his whole person. In form, it may resemble expressive language, but it is not merely subjective.

8. *Ceremonial language*—"How are you?" This kind of language functions as a series of shorthand signals to facilitate social intercourse. It initiates and concludes social contacts: "Hello," "'Bye," "Dear Sir," "Sincerely yours," etc. Thus "How are you?" as ceremonial language is a different *kind* of language than the "How are you?" of interrogative

language. The latter asks for information; the former does not, but serves to facilitate social interaction. We usually perceive this linguistic shift instinctively, and do not respond informationally to the ceremonial "How are you?", and recognize that the speaker (not really "questioner") of "How are you?" in the ceremonial sense should not be charged with phoniness for not wanting to know *too* much about our current state of health, economics, and such. Each language game has its own rules.

9. *Religious language*—"You shall worship the Lord your God, and him only shall you serve." Religious language serves to express our concern with God and ultimate meanings. "Religious language" can be considered to belong to the same series as 1—8 above, or as a separate category overlapping several kinds of language listed above. An adequate categorization and analysis of the various kinds of language is the task of the philosopher of language and thus is beyond my competence. There is presumably more than one legitimate way to make such classifications and analyses. The point here is clear enough, that there *are* such varieties of language which differ from each other in kind.

"Religious language," however it is placed in the series with other types of language, is comprised of subtypes of language. Just as language itself is not one homogeneous entity, so "religious language" is not one uniform "kind" of language but contains a rich variety. John Macquarrie, in analyzing the religious language of St. Athanasius, detected eight subtypes of religious language used by him: myth, symbol, "existential" discourse, "ontological" discourse, metaphysical language, the language of authority, empirical argument, and the language of paradox.[41]

If we are to see that the paradoxical language of the New Testament makes any kind of *sense,* the first task is to be clear that, just as one cannot play "sports" but must play some *particular* game (and to be conscious of *which* game one is playing), so one does not just speak "language" but always some particular kind of language. To become conscious of the variety of kinds of language is the first step towards understanding that the paradoxical language which the New Testament and the classical creeds employ is *one* kind of *valid* language.

The Order of Language and the Order of Being

Reinhold Niebuhr wrote that "All definitions of Christ which affirm both his divinity and his humanity in the sense that they ascribe both finite and historically conditioned and eternal and unconditional qualities to his nature must verge on logical nonsense."[42] Is this what Mark, the other New Testament authors, and the framers of the classical Christian creeds did? Should we understand Mark as saying that the A.D. 30 person, Jesus of

Nazareth, was of such a nature that he was both fully human and fully divine? The New Testament and the creeds are often understood this way today, being rejected (or ignored) as nonsense on the one hand, and zealously affirmed on the other hand, at the price of a *sacrificium intellectus*. But does the language of the Bible and the creeds intend to describe the being of an A.D. 30 person?

Sören Kierkegaard thought so, and much modern talk of paradox has perpetuated his unhelpful way of attempting to handle the problem. For all his talk of the "subjectivity of truth," Kierkegaard believed that the paradoxical language of the New Testament described the nature of the historical person of Jesus. Kierkegaard described the incarnation thus:

> That God has existed in human form, has been born, grown up, and so forth, is surely the paradox *sensu strictissimo,* the absolute paradox.
>
> The object of faith is the reality of another.... The object of faith is not a doctrine.... For it does not concern a doctrine, as to whether the doctrine is true or not; it is the answer to a question concerning a fact: "Do you or do you not suppose that he has really existed?" ... The object of faith is hence the reality of the God-man in the sense of his existence.... The object of faith is thus God's reality in existence as a particular individual, the fact that God has existed as an individual human being.[43]

It is clear that, in using such language, Kierkegaard thinks he is describing the person of the principal figure in an event which really happened in A.D. 30. "God" and "man" are predicates which he affirms without qualification of the Jesus of Nazareth who actually lived. But what can such language mean, when used as though it described the being of the person of Jesus? Given such a view of the church's paradoxical language about Jesus, how would Kierkegaard respond to the fundamental question which has been guiding our discussion: Could such a Jesus have come down from the cross or couldn't he? The logic is clear: If Jesus were really man, he could not have done so; if he were really God, he could have done so. In A.D. 30, historical-Jesus terms, one cannot have it both ways. Kierkegaard recognizes this and attempts to deal with it. In an extended analogy involving a king who loved a peasant maiden and resolved to visit her without disclosing his royal identity, Kierkegaard writes:

> The God has thus made his appearance as Teacher (for we now resume our story), and has assumed the form of a servant. To send another in his place, one high in his confidence, could not satisfy him; just as it could not satisfy the noble king to send in his stead even the most trusted man in his kingdom.... If the God had not come himself ... we would not have had the Moment, and we would have lost the Paradox. The God's servant form however is not a mere disguise, but is actual; it is not a parasitic body but an actual body; and from the hour that in the omnipotent purpose of his omnipotent love the God became a servant, he has so to speak imprisoned himself in his resolve, and is now bound to go on (to speak foolishly) whether it pleases him or no. He cannot then betray himself. There exists for him no such possibility as that which is open to the noble king, suddenly to show that he is after all the

king—which is no perfection in the king (that he has this possibility), but merely discloses his impotence, and the impotence of his resolve, that he cannot really become what he desires to be.[44]

But this is His will, His free determination, therefore an almightily maintained incognito. Indeed, He has in a certain sense, by suffering Himself to be born, bound Himself once for all; His incognito is so almightily maintained that in a way He is subjected to it, and the reality of His suffering consists in the fact that it is not merely apparent, but that in a sense the assumed incognito has power over him.[45]

I quote these extended passages from Kierkegaard because they represent a first-rate mind struggling with the problem of the paradoxical language about Christ, and resolving it in a way which many other Christians have done, though often without Kierkegaard's sophisticated penetration. It boils down to this. Kierkegaard recognizes that in describing the being of the crucified Jesus, he must say either that he "could" or "could not" have come down from the cross. There is no room for double-talk here. But his choice is only relatively clear.

In Kierkegaard's view, the historical Jesus "could not" have come down from the cross, although he was truly divine, because when God decided to enter into human flesh, he decided to suffer for humanity's sake, and it is impossible for God to renounce his own resolve. Kierkegaard has basically a kenotic understanding of the Christ-event, in which the divine incognito plays a very important role. And yet the attempted explanation does not satisfy, as Kierkegaard acknowledges by his parenthetical remarks "to speak foolishly" and "in a certain sense." For his answer remains vague. If one presses for clarity, then this attempted description of the being of the God-Man of A.D. 30 must mean one of two things. It may mean that Jesus "could not" come down from the cross as a matter of his personal integrity, his commitment to himself and the world, not that he, as God, did not have the (meta-) physical power to do so. (In this case Jesus was unlike all other human beings in his death; i.e., he was not truly human.) Or it means that he could not have come down from the cross because of the physical limitations of his humanity. (In this case he was not "God," for God can do this, as is clear from Kierkegaard's discussion that as God he had *resolved* not to do it.) Thus, though clearer than most, Kierkegaard's attempt to explain the meaning of "truly human/truly divine" as a description of the A.D. 30 being of Jesus remains muddled. And since Kierkegaard is the best effort in this regard that we have, or *can* have, we must either abandon such paradoxical language once and for all as meaningless, or understand it in some other way than did Kierkegaard.

Kierkegaard's intent is clear and is to be affirmed: he did not wish to relegate the New Testament's language about Jesus to the world of ideas, to our subjectivity. The New Testament Christological language refers to a person who really lived, to an event which really happened. The church owes Kierkegaard much for rescuing Christological language from the stratosphere of idealistic language and bringing it down to earth in reference to the concrete individual, Jesus of Nazareth. But Kierkegaard's understanding of the nature of language itself was inadequate to his intention and misled him into affirming statements which he should not have made, and need not have. The Kierkegaardian mistake is this: He supposes that the paradoxical Christological language of the New Testament is true only if it describes the being of the A.D. 30 person Jesus. He thus insisted on locating the paradox inherent in the *language* about Jesus in the *being* of Jesus himself. For Kierkegaard it is not just our mode of apprehending the Christ-event which results in paradoxical language; the person and event of Jesus is essentially paradoxical in itself. Paradox is an ontological category.[46] I propose that we would better understand Christological language by locating the paradox in the church's language about Jesus rather than in the being of Jesus, and that this can be done without giving up the claim that Christological language refers to and interprets the event and person of Jesus.

In order to do this, we once again need to clarify our theory of language. We usually tend to suppose that we have no theory of language, that we simple speak in terms that are true or false, in ways that make sense or don't. But as our discussion above of the kinds of language reveals, we do work with an implicit theory of language, a theory which by observing language and reflecting on our observations, can be made less naive and more capable of describing how language actually works.

Most of us probably begin with what has been called the "picture theory" of language. In the "photograph" theory, it is supposed that truthful language communicates reality the way a good camera makes a photograph: by portraying, more or less with 1:1 exactness, what is actually "out there" in reality. Or, to use the alternate metaphor, language "holds up a mirror" to reality and accurately reflects what is "there." If one cannot apprehend reality directly, language will communicate reality, if it is adequate language, in the same way that a photograph or mirror communicates that which one cannot perceive directly. A camera or mirror that distorts reality is no good; so with language. But true language doesn't distort; it just reports "what is."

This commonsense theory of the nature of language seems to work quite well for ordinary occasions. Yet when we examine it closely, we see that even "ordinary" language does not function by simply giving us a 1:1 "photograph" of the way things are. Zeno, the provocative Greek philosopher of the fifth century B.C., enjoyed irritating his associates by pointing out the inadequacies of our ordinary language to describe reality. He devised a number of "paradoxes" to illustrate this, one of the more famous of which is his famous "paradox" of the arrow. (We are here using "paradox" in the general sense.) A flying arrow does not move, Zeno explained, because in order to do so it must move from one point to another. But before it can do this, it must first move half the distance between the two points. But before it can do *this,* it must move half the distance between *these* two points. And so on forever. Not only can the arrow not move, it cannot even get started. Whoever encounters this puzzle supposes at first that this is some parlor game, and that if one thinks about it a moment, he will be able to see the trick and explain it. But is it so simple?

My point here is not to argue whether or not Zeno's "paradoxes" are resolvable but to allow them to point out to us that even our ordinary language, such as "the arrow moves," does not offer us a 1:1 photograph of reality but discloses a gap between language and the reality it points to. For, be it noted, it is only the arrow in Zeno's (and our) *language* that has trouble moving. Real arrows, and a great many other things as well, move right along quite oblivious to the difficulty our way of thinking and speaking has in catching up with them.

This gap between language and being, already perceivable in our language about ordinary things, becomes even more pronounced when we speak of extraordinary things. When we talk of "infinite" or "curved" space and the "black holes" in it, or when we describe the structure of the DNA molecule, we are sometimes painfully aware that our language about the reality we are trying to express is not a mirror image or exact photograph of reality itself. But reality, like the arrow, goes on being whatever it is whether our thought and language is able to express it or not. Things *exist* which can't be expressed in human language, but our failure to be able to describe them apparently doesn't bother them: for example, electrons. Things can be expressed in reasonable, useful language which have no objective existence, such as the square root of minus-one.

So we are talking about two worlds. One is the world of being, the world of what actually is. The other world is the linguistic world, the world of our thought about the world of what is, the world of our attempts to conceptualize and express the world of being. These two worlds, the world of being and the world of language, are not identical. Nor are they related in such a way that the world of (true) language is a photograph of 1:1 mirror-image of the world of being. But they are related. They overlap and affect each other. Neither is independent of the other. In our theory of language the world of being and the world of language must be *distinguished.*

What I am proposing is that we recognize that the paradoxes found in the church's A.D. 70 Christological language in the Gospel of Mark is a phenomenon of language, not of being. The Christological paradox is not to be located in the A.D. 30 person of Jesus (in his *being*) but rather is to be recognized as a paradox located in the A.D. 70 *language* of Mark and other New Testament writers. It seems to me that Christian thought has often taken the wrong fork of the road at this point and located the paradox in the A.D. 30 nature of Jesus. When this has been done, theological language has become a discussion of the hydraulics of the incarnation. But progress in understanding New Testament language about Jesus cannot be made until the paradox is seen not as a 1:1 photographic description of the "two natures" of Jesus, but as a phenomenon of the *language* which Christians properly use in order to express the meaning of the act of *God* in the *Jesus*-event.

This might be represented schematically as follows:

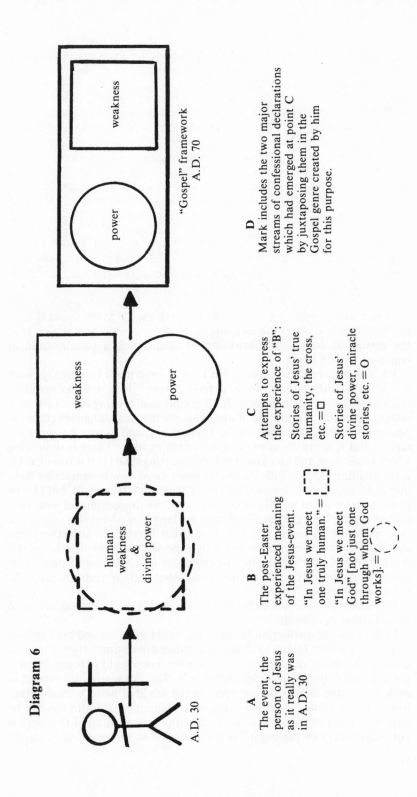

Diagram 6

A
The event, the person of Jesus as it really was in A.D. 30

B
The post-Easter experienced meaning of the Jesus-event.

"In Jesus we meet one truly human." = ⬜ (dashed)

"In Jesus we meet God" [not just one through whom God works]. = ◯ (dashed)

C
Attempts to express the experience of "B":

Stories of Jesus' true humanity, the cross, etc. = □

Stories of Jesus' divine power, miracle stories, etc. = ◯

D
Mark includes the two major streams of confessional declarations which had emerged at point C by juxtaposing them in the Gospel genre created by him for this purpose.

In all of this, ABCD are all related, though not identical. B is mostly logically prior to C, not necessarily chronologically prior, though it may be so. BCD actually flow together in practice but are distinguished for discussion. Each point is dependent on the preceding point in such a way that if A had been different from what it was, B (and hence C and D) would have been different. Yet, B, C, and D do not just offer "photographs" of A but interpret its *meaning* in *language*. In this schema, paradox, Christological language, is the phenomenon of language which emerges clearly at point D, the Gospel form devised by Mark, although it was already implicit in the church's language about Jesus at points C and B. And A was of such a nature that it required both ways of expression present at points B and C, and finally the paradoxical language of D, to reveal its full significance.

In creating the Gospel form, Mark had no intention of attempting to "photograph" or "mirror" the person of the A.D. 30 Jesus. Mark's language is not about the "nature" of Jesus but about the meaning of the Christ-event. This is not a defect and should be no disappointment to us, for most of those who saw the reality of the person and event of Jesus, to the extent that it could be externally viewed in the manner that a photograph or mirror would represent it, *missed* the real meaning. Mark's paradoxical language communicates the meaning of the Christ-event, not the nature of the person of Jesus, for Christological language is a phenomenon of language, not of being.

We may thus begin to perceive the kind of sense made by language such as "Jesus is truly human/Jesus is truly divine." It is not analogous to talking about something *being* both round and rectangular. Talk of a rectangular circle is nonsense, if one supposes that such language claims to describe the *being* of some *object*. There is not, and cannot *be,* any such reality. But it is not nonsense to say something like: "There is something which I can *think* and *talk* about only by asserting that: (1) It is round; (2) It is rectangular; (3) It is fully each; (4) I don't know how to synthesize these disparate, contrary statements into one harmonious statement, but I know that if I surrender or modify either of them I lose the meaning of what I am talking about; (5) I do not claim that my language about this object is a description of its *being,* but I do claim that it refers to something real outside itself which cannot be properly expressed without such language; (6) 'Rectangle' and 'circle' thus function not as photographs or mirror-images of the reality I am trying to express—but as signs, pictures, symbols, not as propositions."

The latter two points have been only hinted at in the preceding, and need to be further developed.

In drawing the distinction between the world of being and the world of language, I do not intend to make an absolute separation between the two worlds. The world of language is *distinct* from the world of being, but it is not separate from it, not independent of it. The two worlds are related in such a way that if anything or event in the world of being were different from what it is, adequate language concerning it would also have to be different. The church's language interpreting the meaning of the event is not independent of the event "as it really was" in the realm of being. By claiming that the church's language about Jesus is not a 1:1 photographic description of the person and event of Jesus, the church does not give up the claim that its Christological language refers to a person and event which really happened, and that it does so in a way appropriate to that event.

Some philosophers of language, still somewhat under the spell of the charges leveled at religious language by logical positivism, have regarded all language as either "referential" (objective) or "emotive" (subjective). The latter purportedly is not talking *about* anything, only expressing the feelings of the speaker and attempting to evoke them in others. Richard Braithwaite, for instance, argued that all religious language functions not by describing transcendent realities, as its surface form appears to suggest, but is basically attitude-evoking rather than referential. From this point of view, the inconsistencies of religious language are no problem, since the contrary statements do not refer to anything. "Indeed, a story may provide better support for a long range policy of action if it contains inconsistencies."[47] Thus the tensions in the church's language about Jesus would be explained as an expected and appropriate element in the church's attempt to express its feelings about Jesus and to invoke attitudes toward him in others.

But this alternative that language *either* objectively refers to something which can be empirically verified, *or* can be reduced to the subjective feelings of the speaker, is a false alternative. When language doesn't objectively describe, it may still do more than subjectively express. This is not a special plea for religious language. The language of poetry, metaphor, and symbol in general often does much more than express the subjectivity of the author. The language of science has no monopoly on the capacity to refer to and mediate the real world. The point cannot be developed and defended here, but has been powerfully argued by Phillip Wheelwright, especially in *The Burning Fountain,* the central thesis of which is that "religious, poetic, and mythic utterances at their best really mean something, make a kind of objective reference, although neither the objectivity nor the method of referring is of the same kind as in the language of science."[48] He argues that poetic language "says something, however tentatively and obliquely, about what is." It is not just emotive but makes "a shy ontological claim" which refers even if it doesn't describe in the photographic or mirror-image sense.[49]

Paradoxical language does not describe, in the 1:1 photographic sense. But neither does it just express the subjectivity of the user. Paradoxical language is the language of the Christian experience, but it is experience *of something.* Paradoxical language points, sign-like, to something beyond itself which cannot be directly described. The experienced meaning of the Christ-event is encountered by the Christian as something which cannot be expressed directly, in logically neat propositional descriptive terms, but which nonetheless must be expressed. It is not just a contentless mystical experience but the experience of the ultimate meaning of something which has happened in history, involving a concrete person who lived and died. When the experienced meaning of the Christ-event is expressed, since the language available is not able simply to directly describe the reality to which it refers, the language functions by pointing, by signifying (*signify-ing*). Though not direct descriptive language, paradoxical language is not without content, for it points in a certain direction and not in others, and it has a certain thrust which excludes some things from being said as the truth, even if it is not able directly to state the truth in nonparadoxical language. Just as children, overwhelmed with something for which they do not have the vocabulary, grammar, and conceptual categories to describe directly still need not be either mute or incoherent but can point to that which grasps their attention, so the church's language about Jesus points beyond itself to the world of reality, without being able directly to represent the reality of that world.

Language and Pictures

Paradoxical language is able to point to the realities of the transcendent world because it is fundamentally picture-language. When Mark has the centurion say "Truly, this man was the Son of God," and when Christians continue to say "Jesus is truly human/Jesus is truly divine," they are not so much making discursive, propositional statements as they are using language which evokes a series of pictures, because language itself is basically pictorial.

A word needs to be said about terminology. The early Wittgenstein thought it necessary that the picture formed in one's mind by reading a statement somehow correspond 1:1 with external reality if the language were to be considered true. This theory of language was thus called the "picture theory" of language. Wittgenstein later abandoned this theory, and spoke of the various functions of language, which use pictures in various ways to express various "forms of life." The term "picture theory" is equivalent to what I have called the "photograph" or "mirror-image" theory of language, in that it thinks language capable of accurately representing the external world the way a crisp photograph represents a landscape.

I think it more appropriate to use the term "picture" only with reference to Wittgenstein's later view of language which abandoned the "mirror-image" or "photographic" view. "Picture" is used here not in the sense of a precise 1:1 representation but more in reference to the imagic power of the mind, which thinks creatively in images. "Picture" connotes more the creativity of the artist with palette and brush, while "photograph" suggests the exact representation of external reality. The former is a "soft focus" term, the latter a "hard focus" term. I am using "picture" and "pictorial" intentionally as a somewhat vague term to embrace aspects of a variety of kinds of related language, including metaphor, parable, paradox, symbol, analogy, myth, model, picture, and story. A precise philosophy of religious language would make the appropriate careful distinctions among these subtypes of discourse, but I am not attempting that here.

I am more concerned to point out the common pictorial element in all the subtypes of the genre, in contrast with that kind of language which attempts to be entirely propositional, discursive, amenable to the laws of logic and

106

mathematics (I say "attempts" because I believe even the most coldly scientific or mathematic language is basically pictorial, because language as such is basically pictorial, and because the human mind is basically pictorial, functioning in images rather than formulae or sentences.) A proposition intends to represent truth not by evoking pictures in the mind, which is done only incidentally, but by precisely presenting its subject matter in words which are univocal (=words which mean only one thing) and in grammatical connections which are clear and logical. Propositional language intends to present statements from which valid inferences can be drawn, the goal being that all grammarians, logicians, and computers would agree on the exact meaning of the statement. The pictorial content of the proposition is minimal and unintentional, and may actually get in the way of communicating what the user of the proposition intends. (Math formulas would be better.) At the other end of the spectrum, the narrative operates by evoking a series of moving pictures in the mind of the hearer or reader. While containing propositional, discursive statements, these are incidental to the pictorial function of the narrative.

In these terms, what is paradoxical language? We have seen that a paradox is not just a single, strange picture but *two* pictures held up simultaneously, two pictures which are in tension with each other.[50] Christological language has not affirmed contrary propositions as much as it has sets of tensive pictures. This is what Mark does. Rather than setting down a series of contradictory or contrary statements about Jesus, he holds up to the reader two sets of pictures: one in which Jesus is a weak human being, and one in which Jesus functions as God himself. Each of the two sets of pictures has its proper claim to point to the truth about Jesus. When they are reduced to concepts and discursive language, they seem to exclude each other, as tends to happen in the creed.

To the extent that the church fathers attempted to transform the pictorial language of the New Testament into the propositional language of discursive philosophical speech, they were working against the grain of the material in their tradition. Their intent in this regard is not clear. To a limited degree, they do employ ontological categories with reference to the being of Jesus.[51] But even if the framers of the Chalcedonian Creed thought they were describing the nature of Jesus in the world of being, and thought they were doing so in discursive, propositional language, they did not do so, for the creed in fact functions as a linguistic phenomenon, delimiting the adequate language to be used in Christological confession.[52] The creed has gone farther in the direction of discursive speech than Mark, who intends to evoke a set of mental pictures rather than a series of deductions.

Conflicting pictures can be held together more readily than conflicting propositions. The Fourth Gospel has no difficulty *picturing* Jesus as both "the Lamb of God, who takes away the sin of the world" (John 1:29) and "the Good Shepherd" (John 10:11), nor do we. If in describing a cylindrical can of soup, one says "the soup can is round" and "the soup can is rectangular," the propositions are nonsense when taken together unless they are somehow mediated. But if one holds up a picture of a soup can taken from the side (which in the two-dimensional photograph would

107

represent the can as a perfect rectangle) and says "This is a picture of a can of soup," and then holds up a picture of a soup can taken from directly over it (which would represent the can as a perfect circle), and says "this is a picture of a can of soup," both statements can stand without qualification or mediation. Of course, the viewer has seen a real soup can himself, from several perspectives, and knows how to put the two pictures together in his mind into one comprehensive picture.

Here my analogy breaks down—though it may still be helpful even here. For the viewer of each picture of the soup can is seeing a reality which exists in the same three-dimensional world as he does, and which he has seen directly from several perspectives. With two different fragmentary representations, though they formally conflict, he has no trouble assembling them into one consistent mental picture of how the soup can "really" is. But if we imagine a two-dimensional person, a resident of a comic strip, who has never seen a can of soup or any other three-dimensional object, confronted with two conflicting two-dimensional pictures, this person can have no way of reconciling the two pictures. Unless he chooses between them, he will have no choice but to continue to affirm both of them, without being able to affirm *how* they are both valid pointers to the reality of a three-dimensional soup can. This, of course, is our situation with regard to religious language in general, and paradoxical language in particular. If talk of God refers to anything, it refers to one who exists on a plane which transcends our three-dimensional space-time world. We can no more imagine (that is, picture in our minds) what this more-than-three-dimensional mode of reality is like than a two-dimensional comic-strip character can imagine what the world of real people is like.

What we have been saying is that religious language in general, and paradoxical language in particular, is necessarily both analogical and fragmentary. Since finite human language cannot directly express the transcendent realities which form its subject matter, it can speak of them only analogically, that is, in pictures derived from this finite space-time world. The terms "circle" and "rectangle" are both only analogical and pictorial when applied to the three-dimensional reality of a soup can, but they are the only terms in which "soup can" can be pictured in two-dimensional language. Since this is the case, it is also true that each two-dimensional picture by itself both represents and *mis*represents the reality it points to, for each picture is not only analogical; it is also fragmentary. No *single* two-dimensional picture can represent the three-dimensional reality. Precisely because of the fragmentary nature of all human language which refers to the transcendent, more than one picture of the same reality is necessary, even though these pictures cannot be harmonized. A truer, more adequate picture of what the ultimate reality is can be obtained by two conflicting pictures than by either alone, or by a single artificially constructed picture which attempts to synthesize their conflicts. Thus, although paradoxical language is necessarily analogical and fragmentary, this is not to be lamented or grudgingly tolerated, because paradoxical language is the appropriate language for talk of ultimacy.

Paradox and the Language of Ultimacy

The penultimate (less than ultimate) things by which we exist, on the level that other animal life exists, can be talked about in ordinary language with ordinary logic without tensions. Loaves of bread can be counted and weighed, and must be dealt with in objective, scientific language. Paradoxical language has no place at the checkout counter at the supermarket. The ordinary logic of ordinary language is the language of business, law, and ordinary conversation which creates and maintains the network of relationships without which we could not exist. The use of paradox does not require that we demean or reject the language world of ordinary logic, for we all live in this world too. Such language must be kept logically and mathematically responsible; budgets must balance. But such inert, objectifying language is for the inert objects of our everyday world. And though we must have bread to live, as *human* beings, we do not live by bread alone (Deuteronomy 8:3; Matthew 4:4; Luke 4:4). And so our language cannot be only that language which is appropriate to penultimate things. Ordinary language, within the confines of ordinary logic, will enable us to exist; but in order to *live,* language must enable us to deal with those ultimates which give meaning to our life (such as love), the meaning of life, death and what may lie beyond it, values, God or the absence of God. Language that deals with life (as opposed to mere existence) must itself be alive.

What does it mean for language to be "alive"? Phillip Wheelwright, who contrasts the "tensive" language that deals with the things by which we ultimately live with the "steno-" language of our ordinary conversation about ordinary things, responds:

> Now what is it for language to be alive? In all organic life there is a ceaseless but varying struggle between opposite forces, and without such struggle the organism would go dead. "Strife is the common condition," Heraclitus remarks, "and if strife were to vanish from amongst gods and men, then their very existence would cease." . . . Thus language that strives toward adequacy . . . is characteristically tensive to some degree and in some manner or other.[53]

Even at the most elementary level, life requires not only bread but the struggle for bread. The language of life is itself caught up in this struggle, and struggles within itself to give voice to those ultimates by which we live. Paradox is the language that corresponds to the ultimate.

The biblical term for "ultimate" is "eschatological." The eschatological events are those final events which bring God's plan for this world to completion. Biblical language that attempts to express these eschatological realities gives us the biblical pictures of salvation (the eschatological deliverance from all the enemies of life), eternal life (eschatological realization of what life struggles to be, the fulfillment of life), resurrection (God's eschatological act of delivering humanity from the apparent victory of death), judgment (God's eschatological righting of wrongs, giving good and evil their just deserts), the church (the eschatological community which already orients its life by God's ultimate purpose, rather than the penultimate values of the transient culture).

The one biblical picture which, for Christians, is the key to all eschatological language is the biblical picture of the Christ (the eschatological king who will bring in the rule of God at the Endtime). All language concerned with such realities is eschatological language, the language of ultimacy. It deals with that which brings the end to our ordinary world, and fulfills it in God's ultimate purpose. The New Testament, of course, is composed principally of just such language, for it witnesses throughout to an event which Christians believe both reveals God's eschatological rule and makes it present in this world.

It is the effort of the finite human mind to express these eschatological realities, focused on the Christ-event, which deforms ordinary logic and results in paradoxical language. Without paradox, the ultimate does not come to expression in finite language. The failure to use paradoxical language, attempting to fit talk of the ultimate into the categories of ordinary logic and language, results in reducing the ultimate to the penultimate, treating the transcendent as a part of our ordinary world, that is, making an idol of it.

Of course, as we have seen, all language of ultimacy is picture language, and the pictures are necessarily taken from the ordinary world. The eschatological judgment of God is expressed—and can only be expressed—in pictures taken from human law courts. The eschatological king, the Christ, is portrayed in images taken from the kingdoms of this world. The ordinary penultimate world provides the images which are then "infinitely qualified" to allow them to communicate the eschatological reality. All language of ultimacy shares this dual quality of drawing its images from this world, but infinitely qualifying them to make them vehicles of ultimacy,[54] so that such language itself may be said to participate in both worlds at once, the "ordinary" and the "ultimate" world. This is what gives it its necessarily paradoxical character.

Paradoxical language, as the language of ultimacy, deals with the realm of what cannot be (directly) said. Surely the question must have been lurking for some time in the mind of even the most patient and benevolent reader: "If so much must be explained about the difficulty of speaking of the ultimate, if it is all so hard and so debatable, *would it not be better concerning ultimate things simply to maintain a respectful and modest silence?*" This commonsense objection is heard from ordinary folk who, having finally lost patience with theologians and preachers, suggest that we give up trying to express the inexpressible, and confine our talk to realms in which we can have at least some assurance that we know what we are talking about. And the objection has been heard from sophisticated thinkers of all climes and centuries, not all of them hostile to religion.

Eastern religion has in general been more modest in its claims to talk about the ultimate. "*Neti, neti*" (Not this, not this) repeats the Buddhist as he confesses the inadequacy of all human concepts and language to express ultimacy. "If you meet the Buddha on the road, kill him," is the motto of one Buddhist group as they radically insist that anything which can be perceived, expressed, or conceptualized cannot be the true Buddha.[55] "The Tao that can be expressed is not the real Tao," said Laotze.[56]

More recently, Ludwig Wittgenstein, near the end of his early period, was challenged by the charge that, if metaphysical statements are all meaningless, then Wittgenstein's own book is meaningless. Wittgenstein's response formed the conclusion of his book:

> My statements are elucidatory in this way: he who understands me finally recognizes them as senseless, when he has climbed out through them, on them, over them. (He must, so to speak, throw away the ladder after he has climbed up on it.) He must surmount these statements; then he sees the world rightly. *Whereof one cannot speak, thereof one must be silent.* [emphasis mine][57]

And Thomas McPherson, in an essay, "Religion as the Inexpressible," declares that "The things that theologians try to say (or some of them) belong to the class of things that just cannot be said," so he suggests that "The way out of the worry is to retreat into silence."[58] Long before them all, Isaiah had written that God's ways were not man's ways, nor God's thoughts man's thoughts (Isaiah 55:8-9), and Paul had declared the realities of the transcendent world to be inexpressible (1 Corinthians 2:9; 2 Corinthians 9:15; 12:4).

"Whereof one cannot speak, thereof one must be silent." The suggestion is not altogether without merit, given the confident prolixity of theologians and the glib effusion of religious-sounding banalities which typifies the cultural cartoon of the preacher, and the easy talk of God and ultimate things so characteristic of cultural Christianity. Silence before the Infinite is not to be disdained (Job 40:3-5; 42:3).

Or, if one cannot be silent, one can still give acknowledgment to the presence of the Infinite, without trying to express it in language. This is what the Eastern mystic (even if he lives in Omaha) does as he meditates among his incense and chants of "O-o-o-m-m-m." This is what some Christian practitioners of glossolalia do, as they give expression (but not linguistic, logos-expression) to the majesty of God.[59] This is what all Christians do in the wordless rituals of worship and sacrament, and in nonliturgical body-language rituals (a hug) which communicate ultimacy and transcendence without giving it linguistic voice.

Should we not simply settle for this? No, we should not. And we cannot. We may deplore the profusion of superficial religious talkativeness, as we observe that celebrity Christians, faith-healers, and "interpreters of Biblical prophecy" not only have their own lucrative TV word-mongering hits but are regulars on the "secular" talk-shows as well. But because we are human beings, we cannot avoid speaking, and speaking about the things which matter most to us. We are linguistic beings, linguistic at the core. I am not, of course, referring to our gossipy enjoyment of talking but to our essential nature: Without words we cease to live as human beings. I speak, therefore I am.

To address us as human beings, ultimate reality must find linguistic expression. And when the eschatological realities come into language, language is necessarily deformed. Ordinary logic, ordinary grammar, steno-language, cannot handle it. The ultimate-that-has-come-into-history, that is, the Christ-event, creates its own linguistic forms. Two of these prominent in the New Testament are parable and paradox.

Much attention has recently been given to the nature of the parabolic speech of Jesus in the Gospels. It is now generally agreed that parables were not just folksy decorations or illustrations for Jesus' teaching which could have been, and was, expressed in ordinary language, but a different *kind* of language. In the parable, ordinary ways of thinking are jolted, deformed, in order to allow transcendence to emerge in the parable itself. The parable is a linguistic event in which the ultimate word of God's kingdom emerges into speech. And when God's kingdom erupts into our lives in the parable, its primary effect is *demolition.*

This has been most clearly expressed in the work of Robert Funk and Dominic Crossan, whose description of the function of parabolic language is here followed.[60] As sinful human beings, we consciously or unconsciously fence ourselves off from the real world of God's kingdom by constructing an artificial mental world which corresponds to our own values, our own way of seeing "how things are." Crossan calls this mental world in which we normally live "myth," though most people would call it the very opposite: the "real" world, the "way things are." We thus live our lives in this self-constructed world, insulated from the realities of God's kingdom.

Our world is well-constructed, fortified against frontal attack. Then comes the parable. The parable at first seems innocent enough, rather enjoyable in fact, and it gains entrance to our mythical thought world because it seems at first to belong to it. But the parable is the subversive advance agent of another kingdom—the kingdom of the God we have defended ourselves against, even by our religion and theology. Unless we are very careful—and perhaps even then—the parable attacks our linguistic world from within, and leaves our mythical world in a shambles. We thought we knew "how things are," we thought the parable belonged to this world of "how things are," and before we quite realized what had happened, we are left standing amidst the ruins of our myths. For the parable opens up the possibility of seeing the truly real world of how things —ultimately, in God's kingdom—in fact *are.* But the parable does not tell us that. The parable subverts the false world but does not deliver the real one into language in any other way than as the parable itself. There is a sense in which the parable is essentially negative.

The Buddhist "Not this, not this" simply rejects all claims to express ultimacy as inadequate. If language about Jesus were expressed in ways that correspond to this common *via negativa* of religious and philosophical speech, the result would be "he is not truly human/he is not truly divine," etc. That is, one would try to safeguard the mystery of the incarnation by rejecting every effort to conceptualize and express it linguistically. The parable has a certain kinship with this *via negativa,* in that it reminds us that every statement, every mental construction of everyday logic that claims to tell us how things ultimately *are* is to be rejected. Paradox is the ally of parable, but not identical with it.

As parable breaks up the crust of our old world and prepares it for the new life of the kingdom of God, paradox attempts to declare the realities of this new life in positive terms. We have seen that this does not, and cannot, happen without paradoxical language. Parable is that form of language which corresponds to the incarnation[61] in its subversive, ground-clearing negation of our falsely constructed world. But paradoxical language, pairs of positive statements in logical tension with each other, is the form of language which corresponds to the incarnation in its constructive reconstitution of our linguistic world. Myth establishes our (false) world. Parable demolishes this world. Paradox establishes the real world: but only as paradox.

For Further Reading

Crossan, John Dominic, *In Parables: The Challenge of the Historical Jesus.* Harper & Row, 1973.

Ferre, Frederick, *Language, Logic, and God.* Collins, 1961.

Funk, Robert W., *Language, Hermeneutic, and Word of God.* Harper and Row, 1966.

High, Dallas M., *Language, Persons, and Belief.* Oxford University Press, 1967.

Macquarrie, John, *God-Talk: An Examination of the Language and Logic of Theology.* SCM Press, 1967.

Ramsey, Ian T., *Religious Language: An Empirical Placing of Theological Phrases.* Macmillan, 1957.

——————, *Words About God: The Philosophy of Religion.* Harper and Row, 1971.

Ricoeur, Paul, *The Rule of Metaphor.* University of Toronto Press, 1977.

Tilley, Terrence W., *Talking of God: An Introduction to Philosophical Analysis of Religious Language.* Paulist Press, 1978.

Van Beeck, Franz Josef, *Christ Proclaimed: Christology as Rhetoric.* Paulist Press, 1979.

Wheelwright, Phillip, *The Burning Fountain.* Indiana University Press, rev. ed., 1968.

Wilder, Amos N., *Early Christian Rhetoric: The Language of the Gospel.* Harvard University Press, 1971.

Wittgenstein, Ludwig, *Philosophical Investigations.* Blackwell, 3rd ed., 1967.

5

The Gospel as Paradox

Paradox and the Language of Religion

When we Christians use paradoxical language to express our faith in God's act in Jesus, we need not feel that we are engaging in some sort of special pleading for the legitimacy of such language. In the preceding pages, I have suggested that wherever we speak of ultimacy, paradoxical language emerges.

Christianity did not invent paradoxical language. Since religion deals with ultimacy, paradoxical language emerges wherever religion comes to speech. "Brahman is both far and near." "Nirvana is peace/Nirvana is not peace." "It stirs and it stirs not." These affirmations[62] from Hinduism and Buddhism concerning ultimate reality testify to the fact that wherever people are religious, language is generated which is in tension with the canons of ordinary logic. This is also true of the particular religious stream from which Christianity emerged, represented by the language of the Old Testament.

The writers of the Hebrew Scriptures did not strive after paradox in the reflective manner of the Eastern religions, intentionally formulating paradoxical propositions in order to affirm the inexpressibility of the ultimate. Rather, the Old Testament speaks easily, almost familiarly, of God and the transcendent world. It has often been noticed that the Old Testament is rich in imagery, functioning in pictures rather than in propositions. It has not been so often noticed that frequently a writer chooses a plurality of images to express the same reality, with no apparent concern for their logical compatibility.

Hosea pictures God speaking to Israel using a series of images in which God's judgment is absolute, certain, and terrible: God is a vicious lion or bear whose rage will not be satisfied until he has totally destroyed Israel (5:14; 13:7-9). Alongside such declarations, Hosea places another series of images, in which the mercy of God is just as absolute, certain, and incredibly compassionate: God's love is so great that he cannot give Israel up. He will not come to destroy but will mercifully win Israel back to himself (2:14-20; 11:8-9).

This dialectic of clashing images persists not only through Hosea but throughout the prophets, and much of the rest of the Old Testament as well. On the one hand, God is the righteous judge, who holds his people absolutely accountable for their covenant responsibilities, and who will bring devastating punishment upon them for their sins. On the other hand, God is the compassionate mother, father, or husband, who takes the responsibility for the salvation of his people wholly upon himself, and who will bring his merciful purpose to fulfillment despite the disobedience of Israel, entirely because of his own faithfulness and love.

Thus juxtaposition of clashing images frequently fades into statements, or pairs of statements, which are logically in tension. Pharaoh hardens his own heart (Exodus 8:15), but God hardens his heart (Exodus 4:21). Both affirmations are made simultaneously in 9:34—10:1: "But when Pharaoh saw that the rain and the hail and this thunder had ceased, he sinned yet again, and hardened his heart, he and his servants. So the heart of Pharaoh was hardened, and he did not let the people of Israel go; as the LORD had spoken through Moses. Then the LORD said to Moses, 'Go in to Pharaoh; for I have hardened his heart and the heart of his servants. . . .'"

One further example: In 2 Samuel 7:1-17, God promises to David and his descendants that they will always rule over God's people. The promise is unconditional, entirely a matter of God's own grace and faithfulness. It is explicitly said that if the Davidic king sins, he will be chastened and disciplined, but the throne will not be taken away from him; Davidic rule will last forever, for the promise is unconditional (vs. 14-16). This unconditional promise is repeatedly reaffirmed: 1 Kings 11:36; 15:4; 2 Kings 8:16-19; 2 Chronicles 21:7. But the editors of the historical books of the Old Testament have included a series of narratives in which the same promise is made to David's house, with one exception: It is entirely dependent upon the obedience of the Davidic kings to God's covenant demands. This conditional version of the promise to David is found in 1 Kings 2:1-4; 6:12; 8:25; 9:4; 11:38. The first series of pronouncements expresses God's sovereignty and mercy, which are unqualified. The second series of statements expresses human responsibility, which is also unqualified. The Old Testament authors obviously did not wish to dilute either God's sovereignty or human responsibility, stated both in absolute terms, and were unconcerned as to how such pairs of statements might square with the canons of formal logic. The language of the Old Testament is unself-consciously paradoxical. Since it speaks of the acts of God in history, the Eternal in time, the subject-matter emerges in language quite naturally as paradox. "For the Bible it takes two to be right."[63]

Paradox and the Language of Science

For the purpose of ordinary scientific description, such as measuring the density of water or calculating the effect of pressure at one point in a hydraulic system on the valves in another part of the same system, ordinary language that does not violate the laws of consistency and coherence must be used. So much of experimental science is of this nature that we sometimes suppose all scientific language is logically neat and precise. But when science begins to deal with the boundaries of its own subject matter, the ultimates which comprise the framework for its usual discourse, paradoxical language emerges. This happens, for example, in the case of the ultimately small (microphysics), the ultimately large (astrophysics, macrophysics), and the effort to describe "dimensional transcendence."

The ultimate building blocks of the universe, the subatomic entities of which all matter and energy are comprised, have been described alternately as particles and as waves. The electron, for example, has sometimes been described as though it were a minute particle in orbit around the nucleus of its atom, in the same way that planets orbit the sun. Alongside the planetary model, the electron has been described in terms of complex wave patterns in which "mass" and "position" could play no role. These are not just alternate picturesque ways of describing electrons which can then be refined in the laboratory to disclose "the way electrons really are." In experiments, electrons must be thought of as exhibiting particle characteristics, *and* wave characteristics, in such a way that no *unified* picture of electrons emerges.[64] "Wavicle" just doesn't do it. In order to talk about electrons at all, scientists must talk about them using both particle-language and wave-language. The same is true in discussion of the nature of light. Niels Bohr, one of the most influential nuclear physicists of our century, has argued that "we must abandon the search for a single picture of the microphysical object and accept a set of mutually exclusive representations."[65]

There are some obvious analogies here to our discussion of paradoxical language in Christology. Scientists realize that their descriptions of the electron do not correspond 1:1 to reality, that they can only use conflicting pictures which fail to do justice to "the way it really is," and *must* do so. Just as is the case with Mark's pictures of Jesus, more than one picture is necessary to say what must be said about the reality, and the pictures cannot be synthesized. In each case, the paradox does not reside in the object to which the language refers. The man Jesus simply was what he was, and electrons are what they are. In each case, the paradox resides in our efforts to describe electrons or the Christ-event in a way that does justice to what must be said. We thus see that the language of Mark and the New Testament about the ultimate reality manifest in Jesus is not so different from the language which science must use to talk about ultimate reality in its most physical sense.

Paradox, Life, and Literature

Poets, dramatists, and novelists have long known that human life itself has a reality which resists expression in any monological, single-perspective, one-thing-at-a-time mode. The meaning of life, as such, the meaning of any individual life, even the meaning of any event or series of events in one person's life, cannot be adequately represented by a narrative presented from only one perspective. Thus some novelists have developed the technique of telling the same story more than once, from the perspective of more than one participant in the story. John Gardner's *Sunlight Dialogues* is a moving example: The reader is aware that he is engaged with transcendent meanings, that ultimate issues are at stake in what is being portrayed in the lives of the characters in the story.[66] But these do not come to expression in any other way than as the fragmentary perspectival apprehensions of truth communicated by each of the characters. The reader becomes aware that the truth of the living situation can't be captured in any one perspective, and that the perspectives can't be synthesized. If one is to have the truth about life at all, he must have it as a collection of irreconcilable fragments. This juxtaposition of irreducible truth-fragments, with all its disruptive character, is what makes literature more than the mere expression of subjectivity but the vehicle of truth.

Paradox and the Language of Love

We use the language of paradox in the most ultimate of all human relationships. The language of love is paradoxical language. Love has an ultimate dimension within human life. It is absolutely foundational. No love, no human life. When we talk of love, we are talking about that which concerns us ultimately. And yet love cannot be directly described or seen. [67] Like all ultimates, it can be expressed only indirectly, as the thousands of love songs, poems, and letters bear witness. Love is not amenable to logic. One cannot respond to the words "I love you" by saying, "Hmm, I can accept that, it seems reasonable enough."

By this I do not intend to give encouragement to that romanticist notion which reduces "love" to body chemistry, passion, subjectivity, feeling. Whatever love is, it is not simply a subjective feeling. It is a relation *between* people, not a feeling *in* them. And the language of love is not only the expression of feelings. When we talk of love, we are talking about *something*. And yet the language of love, without being nonsense, simply is not subject to the ordinary laws of logic. A man can say to his wife, "I love you totally, I love you with my whole being." And he can say the same to his son, his daughter, his mother, his father, his God. The daughter cannot ask,

118

"But do you love me *more* than my brother?" The language of love is not that kind of language. If we limited ourselves only to statements which were strictly logical, the language of love would wither and die, because all language of ultimacy is in tension with logic.[68]

Paradox as the Language of Commitment

Paradox as the language of love is necessarily the language of involvement and experience. We have seen that paradoxical language is in the form of pairs of logically incompatible, but equally necessary, assertions, for which the claim is made that they mediate the truth simultaneously and in tandem. But such logically odd language is not simply a problem to be analyzed objectively. Paradoxical language, seen from inside, is not the problem but the response to a problem. And the problem is not an abstract problem which may be dealt with from the spectator's stance, but an experienced problem which rises up from the depths of human existence: How can one *speak* of that which concerns us ultimately?

One who has never been touched by such human problems, if there be such a one, can only describe the language used by others, and shake his head at the logical difficulties it contains. The one who has never loved or been loved, if there be such a one, can only observe the behavior and language of those who claim to love, and analyze such language in terms which are cool, measured, logically neat. But one who loves finds himself using language which is in tension with logic in order to express what he knows to be real, "logical" or not.

One who was born blind and has never *seen* light cannot have the problem of expressing and describing light, talking about light, in the same way as one who has *experienced* light, *lives* by and in it. For the blind man, paradoxical wave/particle talk about the nature of light (see pp. 117-18) is only a problem to be dealt with hypothetically. For the one who sees and lives by and in light, it is an experienced reality which is not to be denied, even if it cannot be explained. For this one, language about light, even if it must be paradoxical, is a welcome answer to the problem implicit in the experience itself, rather than a problem to be solved.

Paradoxical language emerges out of experience of the ultimate, whether the ultimate be thought of in religious categories or not. The experience is already given. It is not generated by paradoxical language. We find ourselves already involved in the experience of the ultimate simply by living, if we so much as scratch beneath the surface of life. We do not create paradoxical language in order to attain experience of the ultimate; we find ourselves already there, and our efforts to give voice to this necessarily results in language which is in tension with formal logic.

For the laws of formal logic do not allow for experience. Indeed, they are the farthest removed from experience, intended to be uncontaminated by the ambiguities of actual living. Gilbert Ryle's helpful distinction between formal and informal logic is illuminating: Formal logic is comparable to parade-ground marching, geometry, and accounting, not to battle, cartography, and trading.[69] While these are not unrelated, they are not identical.

"The battlefield is not a makeshift parade-ground; and the parade-ground is not a sham battlefield."[70] Troops in battle will perform better because they have been disciplined on the parade-ground; but their movements in battle should not be judged by rules of parade-ground marching. And what we actually experience in the depth of life is the battle, the mapping of irregular contours, the give-and-take of trading. When language emerges to express the reality of these experiences, it must not be criticized from the uninvolved spectator's stance in logic, geometry, and accounting. Paradox is thus one of the varieties of confessional language. It confesses the reality which is already present in experience.

To live fully as a human being is to live in a world which is simply "too much"—too much to be grasped, sorted out, and analyzed logically and neatly. Human life is "threshold existence,"[71] always on the time boundary between the past and the future, always on the threshold between the subjective "I" and the external world, always on the border between the seen and the unseen worlds. Everyday logic and language always flounder when they attempt to express these essential tensions which are the very stuff of our experienced human life. It is not just religious experience that defies reduction to consistent logical categories but human experience as such. When one does describe this in religious terms, it is expressed as the experience of awe, wonder, the Holy, the Other, the Transcendent, that Infinity before which we stand at every moment. Doxological language, worship language, is paradoxical.[72] Apart from the sense of wonder before the world and one's own experience, there is no problem to which paradoxical language is the response, and paradoxical language itself falsely *becomes* the problem.

Whoever is insensitive to his or her own experience of the ultimate in the depths of personal human existence will regard paradoxical language as simply confusion or a failure of nerve in the realm of hard, clear thinking. But this "clarity neurosis"[73] can be healed not by cultivating specifically religious experience but by attending to the depths of our own human existence. At bottom, these are the same.

Paradox makes no sense in abstraction. But then our human lives are never lived in abstraction. We do not live in generalities, even the generalities of "human existence," but only in particulars. Language of whatever sort can only be understood within its situation. Logical positivism mistakenly supposed that a sentence could be examined for its meaning *in abstractio.*

In the preceding chapters we have attempted to show how the particular Christological language of the Gospel of Mark arose. The Gospel of Mark is a historical document, which means that Mark's language simply cannot be understood without understanding something of the historical situation from which it emerged. Mark would never have devised the series of fully human/fully divine images if each had not already been in circulation, contending with each other, and if he had not recognized the value of each and wanted to preserve them both. The language of the Chalcedonian Creed cannot be understood apart from the political, ecclesiastical, regional, and theological struggles of the fourth and fifth centuries. Unless one experiences the problems which these situations dealt with from inside, that is, unless one belongs to the same community of faith which shares this commitment and experience which is involved in the subject matter which comes to expression in paradoxical language, such language will always appear quaint or absurd. To those who do not love, the language of love is frivolous.

All this is to say that, generally speaking, paradoxical language makes sense only inside a particular world of discourse and that one enters this world by becoming conscious of one's ultimate concern. In particular, Christological language makes sense only within the community of Christian faith, and one enters this community by a commitment of faith. Christological language is not observer-language but insider-language, the language of faith. This does not mean that one must already be a believer before one can be grasped by paradoxical language. But to *understand* such language, one must understand what kind of language it is, the appropriate language within a committed community of faith.

It should also be clear by now that "faith" in this regard does not mean anything like closing one's eyes in the face of logical absurdities and saying through clenched teeth, "I believe anyway." It is not a matter of working at believing impossible things before breakfast. Rather, what is implied here is that there is a structure of knowledge which is implicit in faith itself, as Rudolf Bultmann argues on the basis of Paul.[74] "Knowledge" is not something that exists in abstraction but is a function of the knowing human self. And this self cannot be a neutral spectator before the ultimate but is always already committed one way or the other. In Romans 8:5-9 Paul explains that there is knowledge which is *kata sarka* ("according to the flesh," i.e., this-worldly knowledge measured by this-worldly standards) and knowledge which is *kata pneuma* ("according to the Spirit," i.e., knowledge mediated by encounter with the eschatological event and perceived by the working of the eschatological gift of God's Spirit).

This means that the paradoxical language of the Christian faith is always the language of decision. It is the language of a community which lives by a decision already made and constantly remade. Such language expresses the decision of the believing individual, and is a constant call to decision. It is at the farthest pole from hypothetical language.

Mark also knows this, and would teach us this about his own use of language. In Jesus' encounter with the virtuous rich man in Mark 10:17-27, Jesus first refuses the "divine" accolades which are offered him, divorcing himself from "divinity" and placing himself entirely within the human category (vs. 17-18). But then Jesus makes an ultimate, absolute claim on the man's life, a claim which only God has a right to make—as Jesus has been doing from the first page of Mark's Gospel. The transcendent is met in the ordinary, the divine in the human. The "truly human/truly divine" language about Jesus is implicit in this pericope.

The disciples had anticipated that such a prize "catch" as this man would surely be welcome in the kingdom of God, for he not only had riches, the sign of "success" and God's blessing, and had always kept the commandments, but with all this he was aware of his lack and not too proud to inquire of an itinerant carpenter-preacher concerning eternal life. A good man this, and we share the disciples' consternation when Jesus pronounces it "impossible" for the man to be saved, as impossible as for a camel to go through the needle's eye. We can join in the disciples' uneasy response, "Then who can be saved?" which is the cue for the punch line of the story: "With men it is impossible, but not with God; for all things are possible with God" (v. 27).

In this story, Mark calls for a decision between two ways of thinking and speaking (v. 27). The first way he calls *para anthropois* ("with men"). This refers to a purely this-worldly, human orientation for one's thinking, corresponding to Paul's *kata sarka* ("according to the flesh"). The second way Mark calls *para to Theo* ("with God"). This way of thinking reckons with the act of God which seems utterly camel-through-needle's-eye impossible when thought of from a human point of view, a way of thinking which corresponds to Paul's *kata pneuma* ("according to the Spirit"). Mark also presents these two alternative ways of thinking in the key scene in 8:27-33, especially the climactic 8:33, to which 10:27 is parallel.

A decision is called for here, a step of commitment into the circle of faith. The biblical word for this, the Markan word for it, the word which has characterized Jesus' call since his opening words in Mark 1:15, is *metanoia,* "repentance." "Repentance" in the Bible never has the popular meaning of being somewhat chagrined that one has done some wrong things. The word means literally a change *(meta)* of mind *(noia.* cf. *noeo,* "think," and *noema,* "mind.") Repentance is a new way of thinking, a new way of perceiving how things are. In Mark, whoever would follow Jesus (v. 21), inherit eternal life (v. 17=enter life; 9:43, 45), enter the kingdom of God (v. 25), and be saved (v. 26) must change his or her way of thinking, must step out of the ordinary *para anthropois* world of thinking-speaking-living where what is impossible to think, speak, and live *happens* because of the incursion of God into the human world.

If the world proclaimed, lived, and met in Jesus is the real world, as Mark believes, and not just an illusion, then this world can only be talked about paradoxically. Paradoxical language is the language of ultimacy, the language of the kingdom of God, and thereby necessarily the language of experience, involvement, confession, worship, faith, decision. It belongs to a world which we enter only by repentance, but it is the native language of that world.

Paradox, Human Finitude, and Sin

We come now to a point which could have been appropriately developed in relation to the discussion concerning paradox as the appropriate language for ultimacy (pp. 109-113). The subject matter to which paradox seeks to give expression is the ultimate, the infinite. But the corresponding point is that the subject who makes paradoxical affirmations is a finite self. I have reserved this discussion for this point in order to relate it to the immediately preceding section concerning *metanoia,* for paradox is the language of repentance. That is, paradox is the appropriate linguistic mode for acknowledging one's self to be a finite creature, not the creator of the universe, not the highest mind in the universe, not the center of the universe, not even the measure of the universe. Paradox is not only the appropriate form for the expression of ultimate subject matter; it is the appropriate form of expression for finite beings who confess, in the religious sense, their finitude. In this form of expression, "finite-beings-who-talk-about-ultimacy" and who necessarily do so only in the broken language of paradoxical statements, there is something which corresponds to the Christological paradox of eternity-in-time, the ultimate revealed in the finite.

From Genesis 3 onward, when humanity yielded to the serpent's attractive suggestion that we need not remain the tillers of Someone Else's garden but could assert ourselves and "be like God, knowing..." (Genesis 3:5), we human beings have been reluctant to admit that our own minds are not ultimate. There have been many commonsense assertions that "if it is not logical (i.e., doesn't fit the way my finite human mind thinks), then it is simply not true." We all, by virtue of our common Adamic humanity, have something of this in us. We all still participate in the *kata sarka* world (Paul); we all can still identify with the disciples who continue to think *para anthropois* (Mark). We still don't like to admit that our minds are limited, much less twisted, but the acknowledgment of precisely this is one aspect of repentance, that shift in the orientation of our thinking from the mundane world as ultimate to the eschatological reality manifest in Christ as the point of orientation for our thinking.

The speaking self is a finite self, whose perceptions are fragmentary; this much must be said without regard to religious speech. The speaking self is a sinful self, whose perceptions are distorted; this much must be said from the point of view of the Judeo-Christian faith. When something is declared to be "self-evidently" true or false, the nature of the self making such judgments should be kept in mind.

Some key passages in 1 Corinthians poignantly express this Christian perspective, for the major issue between Paul and the Corinthians was the extent to which the Christian message was to be subject to the canons of Corinthian *logos kai sophia* ("logic/language and wisdom"). The Corinthians listened to the teaching of Paul, Apollos, and Peter, three teachers of the Christian message. Since these three spoke from different perspectives, their interpretation of the gospel was diverse. The ultimate truth of the gospel can never be presented absolutely, that is, in terms of a system of thought which is unconditioned by the relativities of human thinking, but will always appear within the finite human thought systems of its representatives. There is one gospel, but the gospel must necessarily be expressed in some system of thought, so there are numerous theologies. The finitude and fragmentariness of the human situation cannot be detoured in order to present the gospel in some "pure" form uncontaminated by human thought and speech. There is thus a plurality of theologies bearing witness to the one gospel. This is Paul's view: In the world of the Spirit, there may be more than one valid system of *logos* (logic/language), for several different this-worldly systems of thought may be used to mediate and point to the ultimate truth of the gospel, without any of them claiming to represent it directly.

The Corinthians, on the other hand, suppose that their *logos kai sophia* is a direct representation of the transcendent truth, so that they must choose among conflicting claims to truth. This had in fact happened, with the result that some Corinthians followed Peter, some Apollos, some Paul, etc. (1:12ff.). Paul considers such thinking to be a mark of belonging to *this* world with its pretentious claims to knowledge. Paul is aware that his own theology is different from that of Peter and Apollos, and that these latter two also disagree with each other, but considers that way of thinking which insists that one must choose one and reject the others to be a false logic, a this-worldly "wisdom." Although the Corinthians don't realize it, "all things" belong to them: Peter, Apollos, Paul, and other ways of communicating the one gospel as well (1 Corinthians 3:21-33). Even though they cannot be logically reconciled within one intellectual system, they all bear legitimate witness to the one gospel.

There *are* ways of attempting to express the faith which Paul rejects, as 2 Corinthians 10—13 makes clear. Paul is no advocate of an absolute relativism which regards all claims to truth as equally right and equally wrong. *This* is not the result of insisting on the finitude of the human mind and human understanding. But the limitations of human knowledge and expression make way for a plurality of ways of expressing the one gospel, even when those ways cannot be conceptually reconciled with each other.

Paul presses this point especially in discussing the claims to immediate knowledge of the transcendent world supposedly manifest in the charismatic gifts of "prophecy," "tongues," and "knowledge." In 1 Corinthians 13:8 he points out that *all* present knowledge, inspired and uninspired, will "pass away" (that is, that it participates in *this* world which is not ultimate and which will give way to the world to come). In 1 Corinthians 13:9 he points out that it is "imperfect" (that is, fragmentary, never grasping the *whole* truth). In v. 11 he compares all present knowledge, inspired and uninspired, to the speech and thinking of a baby, so that present knowledge is to eschatological knowledge as a baby's knowledge is to that of a mature adult. The climactic summary of Paul's position is concentrated in 13:12: "For now we see in a mirror dimly, but then face to face. Now I know in part; then I shall understand fully, even as I have been fully understood."

Against radical skepticism, Paul asserts that we do now know. We are not absolutely ignorant of ultimate, transcendent things, because the ultimate has revealed its nature in the Christ-event. It is a false humility, a rejection of the act of God in Christ, to take refuge in agnosticism and respond to all ultimate questions with a shrug or a "Who knows?" We *know*.

Against the confident claim of the Corinthians that this-worldly human knowledge is absolute, to the logical framework of which all claims to speak of ultimate truth must be subject, Paul insists that all knowledge of whatever sort is fragmentary. For Paul, transcendent reality is not simply *opaque,* so that the only proper response to it is silence. But neither is it *transparent,* as Fundamentalism generally believes, so that we can speak

Diagram 7

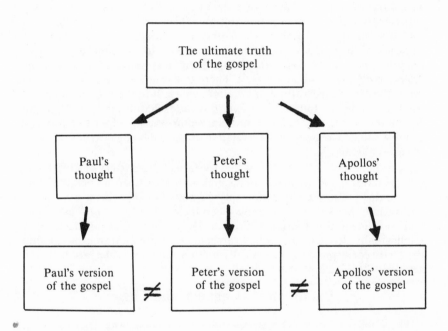

directly and univocally of it in terms which are ultimately logical. (Fundamentalism and Rationalism are siblings, if the former is not simply a version of the latter.) Rather, transcendent reality is *translucent,* perceived "through a glass darkly." Though not totally opaque, it is not totally clear either. (To be clear would in this case be to distort.) But language about the transcendent is not just arbitrary and subjective. It must correspond to what is seen, albeit "darkly," in the Christian revelation. We know *in part.*

But this is not the last word. Paul contrasts this situation "now" when we see only "through a glass darkly" with the eschatological "then" when we shall apprehend the final truth. *Until* then, paradoxical language is necessary in order to speak of the ultimate. But paradox itself is not ultimate, but a by-product of our finitude. There is One who already knows eschatologically, who already has perfect knowledge, who has no need of a plurality of theologies held in tension or of paradoxical language. But *we* are not *God,* and *now* is not *then.* This "then" keeps Paul's discussion from simply glorying in human finitude. There *is* ultimate knowledge. We don't have it yet, in fullness, though we already have it in the fragmentary way appropriate to the human situation. But the eschaton shall *vindicate* our present knowledge as true (though fragmentary) knowledge of what *is.* It is not just subjective, or absolutely relative. It is already engaged with the way things really are.[75]

To the one who still asks "How?" in the face of the mystery of Christ, and insists on fitting the mystery into his present finite categories before he will believe it, Paul has a one-word reply: "Fool!" (15:36). This is not simply frustration, the switch to invective when logic runs thin. "Fool" carries its Old Testament connotation (Psalm 14:1) of one who is not necessarily intellectually deficient, but whose arrogance before God in insisting that the Deity correspond to this-worldly human standards if he is to be taken seriously is its own punishment.

Paradoxical Language and Logic

There has been a wholesome hesitation about the legitimacy of paradoxical language. Gilbert Ryle, in his 1946 inaugural lecture as Professor of Metaphysical Philosophy at Oxford, spoke for many when he argued that "paradox" is a sure indication of confused argument or speech, equated it with "absurdity," and contended that it is a sure way of showing the falsity of an argument. A section of his address is entitled "The Diagnosis and Cure of Paradoxes," suggesting that paradoxical language is to be regarded as "sick," more of a patient than a criminal.[76] More sympathetically, Ronald Hepburn's book-length treatment of the subject still suspects that theologies which rely on paradoxical language "are exposed to a variety of logical objections which render them untenable."[77]

Christian theologians have sometimes been too willing to provide grounds for such suspicion. Since the second century, Tertullian's purported motto, *credo quia absurdum est* ("I believe because it is absurd"),[78] has not only provoked the scorn of outsiders but has also occasionally become the model of Christian discourse for some insiders. In the sixteenth century, Luther refused to submit his faith-statements for judgment by reason, "the blind whore of the Devil."[79] In the last century Sören Kierkegaard wrote in his journal concerning his own theological task that "it was intelligence and nothing else that had to be opposed."[80] In our own time, Karl Barth's great commentary on Romans is in this tradition. In the context of Barth's discussion of the nature of faith, God's promise to Abraham is called "unreasonable," as are all the promises of faith. "Faith, however, is completely abreast of the situation. It grips reason by the throat and strangles the beast."[81]

Whatever Tertullian, Luther, Kierkegaard, and Barth intended—and the above excerpts, frequently taken out of context, do not do justice to the whole position of any of the four—such unguarded defamations of reason tend to suggest that whoever comes into the church must leave his or her reason at the door. From such a perspective, acknowledging the legitimacy of paradoxical language appears to grant a license to talk nonsense. Intelligent, honest persons within and outside the Christian faith are properly reluctant to do this. Christian thinkers do not wish to engage in special pleading, as though the Christian faith were a weakling in intellectual circles and so must be permitted to play by special rules.[82]

I have attempted to show in the preceding discussion of the language of Mark and of Christological language in general that the language of Christian faith is anything but nonsense. By explaining *what* it is and what it is not, and by explaining *why* truth can sometimes be expressed only by using pairs of conflicting statements, paradoxical language can explain, in logical terms, its own nature and necessity. Paradoxical language cannot retreat from giving such an account of itself. It is not immune from responsibility before the bar of reason. No Christian thinker can ever appeal to "paradox" as a *substitute* for hard thinking. Paradox cannot be a catch-all term to excuse sloppy thinking. Paradoxical language comes at the end of a rigorous thought process, not as an alternative to it. And in this, Tertullian, Luther, Kierkegaard, and Barth would all agree.

The relation of the language of Christian faith to the norms of formal logic is a large and complicated subject, beyond both my own competence and the space available in this small book. In closing this discussion, however, I should like to venture some theses as suggestions for further thought. These are directed particularly toward those readers who may be attracted by the language of Mark and the New Testament which speaks of Jesus in terms of both divinity and humanity, but who may be hesitant to use such language because it seems to be in conflict with sound logic.

1. *Logic is not ontological.* When paradoxical language is in tension with logic, *what* it is in tension with needs to be clear. Logic is the term used for the laws of thought. The laws of thought are conceptual, in the mind. Logic, like grammar, is a description of the way human linguistic-conceptual processes actually normally *do* work, rather than a prescription for how they *must* work if they are to be considered "true." This is the view presupposed in the entire preceding discussion. Whether the laws of logic

extend beyond the laws of thinking and speaking about what is, so that they also represent the laws for what actually is, is a disputed point among logicians and philosophers.[83] Aristotle held that the laws of thought were laws of being as well. Kant confined all such laws to the world of thought. Each has his followers today, so that there is nothing more passionate than the debates among logicians on such issues. This brings me to my next thesis:

2. *Logic is not a monolith.* Logic is not a static discipline but a growing realm of knowledge in which new insights call for the revision of older theories. A popular introductory textbook for a course in logic gives examples of arguments which were once considered true, but illogical, but are now considered both true and logical.[84] Statements existed which were perceived to be certainly true, although it was not understood *how* they could be logically true. Then, with more intellectual work, logic caught up with truth. What was once "obviously true," though accepted as true on the basis of something other than logic because it was logically unacceptable by the canons of logic prevailing at the time, was later seen to be logical as well. This shows that logic is not only a descriptive science (rather than a normative one) but that it is an expanding science, able to revise itself in the light of new data, just as do the other sciences. In any given time, logic is thus partial, incomplete, and may later find itself having to revise or deny the "laws" (theories) by which it presently operates. The "New Logic" of Alfred North Whitehead and Bertrand Russell came into being as an effort to secure the foundations of mathematics, which had been developing new concepts and putting them into practice, finding that they "worked," without adequate clarification of the conceptual foundations which support this new superstructure. That is, logic was forced to revise itself to accommodate new truth which had already proven itself on other grounds.

Since the history of logic contains instances in which the perception of truth outran for a time our ability logically to explain how such things could be true, it is perfectly *logical* to believe that there may be truth which must be expressed but with which logic will *never* in this world catch up, because of the limitation of the human mind and human language as such. All of this is certainly not intended to encourage a theology which depends on a "God-of-the-(logical)-gaps." Such pseudo-apologetic has no more place in logic than in physics. The validity of Mark's paradoxical language about the Christ-event does not depend on our being able to find gaps in logical theory. But we do need to see that the logic with which paradoxical language is in tension is itself a growing science constantly in the process of being emended.

It is also helpful to know that logic is not a uniform science but that a variety of logical systems exist. Actually, there is no such thing as "logic" in some absolute sense; there are only various systems of logic which are not compatible with each other. Some of these systems are able to accommodate inconsistent statements without destructive consequences for the system as a whole.[85] Thus logic is no eternally unchanging system but a developing science within which a variety of opinion exists, as are the other sciences that are the product of finite human minds—among which theology is to be counted.

3. *Logic does not deal with historical events.* "Logic is language about language, not language about things or events," says S. I. Hayakawa.[86] "Logic has nothing to do with history," says George Boas. [87] The point of these rather extreme-sounding statements from writers who consider themselves to be logicians, linguists, and philosophers of language rather than theologians, is both clear and important: Logic deals with formal relations between statements, with the world of ideas, not with the historical world of time and space in which things happen. *But the Christian faith deals with the world of things and events, not with the world of ideas alone.* The Christian gospel is good *news,* about something that *happened,* in the real world of time and space. It is not good advice or a good theory. It is not a philosophy, not even in the popular sense of "philosophy of life." It touches down in the empirical world, was nailed down there on a cross. The language which Mark and other Christian thinkers found they must utilize to express the significance of that event is paradoxical. One can have a paradox-free theology if one is willing to (1) limit oneself strictly to one system of thought, call this "the" logic, and consider all other systems to be illogical, and (2) if one is willing to restrict oneself to this world of *ideas,* never allowing them to make contact with the world of things and history. But this is the only way.

Thus the choice of the beginning point of one's thinking and speaking is crucial. If one begins with (conventional) logic as the ultimate norm for all truth and attempts to fit the language of Mark and the New Testament into it, Christology will be sacrificed to logic. This will finally be true of God-talk as such, if by "God" we mean the biblical God who is involved in the world and who acts in history. For there is no way to get from the rules of formal logic to declarations that God (or anyone else) has actually done something in history. But what if one *begins* with the Christian confession as *given,* the confession that in the *man* Jesus *God* has acted for our salvation, and asks what kind of logic and language is appropriate for this confession? It might then become apparent why Mark—and the biblical authors in general—choose the narrative mode of discourse about a historical figure as the vehicle for his faith, rather than the logical or philosophical essay. Christian faith begins with the Christ-event, and tries to find appropriate language for it, rather than beginning with logic and supposing it can infer what must have been. This leads to our next thesis:

4. *Paradoxical language is not part of a formal inferential system.* In ordinary formal logic, if a statement is true, then all that can be legitimately inferred from the given statement is also true. Rigid laws are supposed to govern what can and what cannot be properly inferred from a given statement, laws which are considered to be "completely mechanical."[88] If what can be legitimately inferred from a statement is false, then the statement itself must be false. So, in conventional logic, when a statement is

129

affirmed to be true or false, a mass of dependent inferences is affirmed or denied at the same time.

It is this inferential aspect of conventional logic which finds fault with the paradoxical language used of the Christ-event in the New Testament and the classical creeds. Assuming that what is fully human cannot in the same respect be fully divine, "Jesus is truly human" makes it impossible to say "Jesus is truly divine," and vice versa. There is thus no way, within the inferential structure of conventional logic, to say *both* "Jesus is truly human" and "Jesus is truly divine," although there is no *logical* objection to either statement in isolation.

Likewise, it is the attempt to deal with Christological statements within the inferential structure of conventional logic which has led to heretical, but quite logical, developments of Christological language. *If* the view that "Jesus is truly divine" be granted, *then* certain inferences seemed necessarily to follow: he could not be ignorant, he could not suffer, he could not die. Thus arose a docetic Christology. *If* it be granted that "Jesus is truly human" is true, *then* it was inferred that he was not eternal, not pre-existent, not divine. Thus arose an ebionite Christology. Both views operated within the confines of conventional logic, supposing that Christological statements are amenable to such inferential treatment.

But we have seen that Christological statements are picture-language, analogical language, which sign-like point to the truth without claiming to reflect it in any 1:1 manner. Such statements can mediate ultimate truth, but not in a way that the statements themselves become premises in a system of inference. What the statements *say* may be true, without what they seem to infer, by the canons of conventional logic, being true. In this way they are like the confessional language of worship, miracle stories, prayer, and thanksgiving for answered prayer. The statements of Christ-ological language are confessional language, doxological language, which, in terms of inference-potential within conventional language, function as final statements. They mediate truth in what they *say,* but not in what they may be taken to *imply.* This is the nature of confessional and doxological language.[89] It is not the kind of language which can form the basis for a chain of inferential statements. If such inferences are made anyway, they will surely be wrong: "If you are the Son of God, come down from the cross."

* * *

So we return to the question with which we began, and in the light of the preceding discussion may now summarize our conclusions in response to it.

1. Jesus of Nazareth, the historical person of A.D. 30, was a truly human being who shared our human weakness at the point of death. He could not have come down from the cross. This is an indispensable element in Christian faith.

2. Mark used ordinary language which characterizes other human beings to portray the humanity of Jesus (chapter two above).

3. Mark also used the "divine man" miracle-story language (chapter one above).

130

4. Mark himself does not subscribe to the "logic" of this language. That is, he does *not* consider it legitimate to infer from the miracle-story language, legitimately used to confess faith in God's act in Jesus, that at the point of death he was able, by his divine power, to descend from the cross. "If as the Son of God he could walk on water, then as the Son of God he could come down from the cross" appears quite logical, but it is the logic of the chief priests, not Mark. Thus, not only the historical Jesus of A.D. 30 but the Jesus portrayed in Mark 15:20-39 was not able to descend from the cross.

5. But just as Mark does not infer forward from 6:48 that a Jesus who walks on the water could come down from the cross, he does not infer backward from 15:29-34 that a Jesus who could not come down from the cross could not have walked on the water. We have seen that Mark uses both kinds of language about Jesus, although he does not fit them together into one inferential system.

6. Mark's use of language is not simple. We have had to engage in hard thinking in order to perceive the profundity of Mark's theological accomplishment. This does not mean, of course, that Mark was a philosopher of language who consciously reflected on the nature of paradoxical language. He saw what needed to be said to communicate the wholeness of the church's faith in God's act in Jesus, and devised a profound way to say it in narrative form.

7. Mark's paradoxical language is the language of orthodoxy. Although Mark was not thinking in the categories of the later Nicene and Chalcedonian creeds, they were in their time the proper development and expression of the same paradoxical faith to which Mark gives linguistic form. Heresy, on the other hand, is the result of an undue desire for simplification and a false kind of clarity and logical consistency. Each half of the Christological paradox, if logically and consistently extended in isolation, is heretical. Mark and classical orthodoxy hold together what is heretical if affirmed in isolation. Thus the necessity of dialectic, of the Gospel form created by Mark to embody dialectic in narrative form, and finally the necessity for more than one Gospel. The heretical groups tended to have just one consistent Gospel in their "New Testament." The orthodox mainstream insisted on the more difficult path of canonizing four Gospels which could not be harmonized with each other.

8. The paradoxical language we have discovered in Mark is not a Markan peculiarity. It is not an eddy in the linguistic stream of early Christianity but the main channel. Dealing with it is not optional but is central to the task of grasping the language and theology of the New Testament.

We are finite. Our minds and language are finite. If we will speak of God and his acts, of Christ and his salvation, we will find ourselves talking paradoxical language. The alternative is to fit God into our finite ways of thinking, that is, to make him into an idol. One reason idols are worshiped is that they are neat. When we speak of Christ we will not presume that we have captured his being in our language. We will know that the paradox resides in our talk and not in Christ. But we will know that we are following the linguistic path prepared for us by Mark, the New Testament, and the classical Christian creeds.

For Further Reading

Barbour, Ian G., *Myths, Models, and Paradigms: A Comparative Study in Science and Religion.* Harper & Row, 1974.

——————, *Issues in Science and Religion.* Prentice-Hall, 1966.

Black, Max, *Models and Metaphors: Studies in Language and Philosophy.* Cornell University Press, 1962.

Crossan, John Dominic, *The Dark Interval: Towards a Theology of Story.* Argus, 1975.

——————, *Cliffs of Fall: Paradox and Polyvalence in the Parables of Jesus.* Seabury, 1980.

——————, *Raid on the Articulate: Comic Eschatology in Jesus and Borges.* Harper and Row, 1976.

Ferre, Frederick, *Language, Logic, and God.* Collins, 1961.

Hepburn, Ronald W., *Christianity and Paradox: Critical Studies in Twentieth-Century Theology.* Pegasus, 1966.

Kermode, Frank, *The Genesis of Secrecy: On the Interpretation of Narrative.* Harvard University Press, 1979.

O'Grady, John F., *Models of Jesus.* Doubleday & Co., 1981.

Ramsey, Ian T., *Models and Mystery.* Oxford University Press, 1964.

Slaate, Harold A., *The Pertinence of the Paradox.* Humanities Press, 1968.

Van Buren, Paul M., *The Edges of Language: An Essay in the Logic of a Religion.* Macmillan, 1972.

Notes

1. The information and quotations are taken from David R. Cartlidge and David R. Dungan, *Documents for the Study of the Gospels.* Fortress Press, 1980, pp. 205-42.

2. The majority of New Testament scholars regard Mark as the earliest Gospel. This is the view assumed in this book as the best working hypothesis. I would also claim that the argument of this book offers additional support for this hypothesis. For the major alternative view, that Mark is dependent on both Matthew and Luke, see William R. Farmer, *The Synoptic Problem,* Macmillan, 1964; and *Jesus and the Gospel,* Fortress Press, 1982.

3. Eduard Lohse, *Grundriss der Neutestamentliche Theologie.* Verlag Kohlhammer, 1974, p. 112. [Translation by M. Eugene Boring.]

4. See Reinhold Niebuhr, *The Nature and Destiny of Man.* Charles Scribners' Sons, 1943, Vol. II, pp. 1-15.

5. Elie Wiesel, *Night.* Avon, 1960, pp. 63, 112.

6. Günther Bornkamm, *Jesus of Nazareth.* Harper & Row, 1960, p. 25.

7. Harold von Hofe, *Die Mittelstufe.* Holt, Rinehart and Winston, 1961, p. 124.

8. C. H. Dodd, "The Appearances of the Risen Christ: An Essay in Form Criticism of the Gospels" in *Studies in the Gospels,* ed. D. E. Nineham. Blackwell, 1955, p. 24.

9. Thus those studies of Mark which have regarded the evangelist as only the *opponent* of the "divine man" Christology have not seen the whole picture. An example of this approach is Theodore J. Weeden, *Mark: Traditions in Conflict.* Fortress Press, 1971. On this issue, I am more in agreement with the point of view of Jack Kingsbury, *The Christology of Mark's Gospel.* Fortress Press, 1983, p. 76: "... the attitude Mark invites the reader to adopt toward the miraculous activity of Jesus is one that is positive and not one that is fraught with reservations about a false theology of glory."

10. As quoted in David Hume, *Dialogues Concerning Natural Religion,* ed. Norman Kemp Smith. Thomas Nelson, 1947, p. 198. Cf. Augustine, *Confessions,* VII, 5.

11. This and similar literature from the early church can be read in M. R. James, *The Apocryphal New Testament,* Oxford, 1924; or Edgar Hennecke and Wilhelm Schneemelcher, *New Testament Apocrypha,* Westminster Press, 1965.

12. This and similar literature from the Gnostic movement within and outside early Christianity may be read in Marvin W. Meyer, editor, *The Nag Hammadi Library.* Harper and Row, 1977.

13. *Ibid.,* p. 332.

14. Donald M. Baillie, *God Was in Christ: An Essay on Incarnation and Atonement.* Charles Scribners' Sons, 1948.

15. Martin Kähler, *The So-Called Historical Jesus and the Historic Biblical Christ.* Fortress Press, 1964, p. 80. The original German edition was published in 1896.

16. R. H. Lightfoot, *The Gospel Message of St. Mark.* Oxford University Press, 1950, p. 11.

17. Rudolf Bultmann, *Theology of the New Testament.* Charles Scribners' Sons, 1951, 1955, Vol. II, p. 175. Bultmann here reflects the view of both Luther and Calvin.

18. As quoted in Ian Macpherson, *The Burden of the Lord.* Abingdon Press, 1955, p. 35. Cf. Reinhold Niebuhr, *The Nature and Destiny of Man.* Charles Scribners' Sons, 1964, Vol. II, pp. 287-321.

19. No copies of Marcion's own works have been preserved, but his views are reported in Irenaeus, *Against Heresies,* I, 27:2 and Tertullian, *Against Marcion,* III, 11.

20. These and others may be read in M. R. James, *The Apocryphal New Testament,* Oxford University Press, 1924; and Edgar Hennecke and Wilhelm Schneemelcher, *New Testament Apocrypha,* Westminster Press, 1965.

21. In the remainder of this study, I will use "docetic" as the simplified label for that general type of Christology which affirmed Jesus' divinity but minimized his humanity, and "ebionite" for that type of Christology which emphasized Jesus' humanity at the expense of his divinity. The Christological struggles of the fifth century which gave us the classical formulation "truly human and truly divine" were not actually struggles between Docetism and Ebionism, which were second-century Christian heresies. Rather, the debate at the Council of Chalcedon (A.D. 451) was between representatives of the Alexandrian school which tended toward the docetic view of Jesus at the expense of his true humanity, and representatives of the Antiochene school which, though it was not related to the earlier Ebionite group, did tend to emphasize Jesus' humanity in such a way that the affirmation of a true incarnation of God was threatened. Though technically imprecise, I will use "docetic" and "ebionite" as convenient labels for these two views, as does Karl Barth, *Church Dogmatics.* T. & T. Clark, 1956, IV/1, p. 136.

22. See Frederick Dale Brunner, *A Theology of the Holy Spirit.* Eerdmans, 1970, pp. 285-319.

23. Aristotle, *Magna Moralia* II, 1208b, as cited in Jürgen Moltmann, *The Crucified God.* Harper & Row, 1974, p. 268.

24. Sören Kierkegaard, *Philosophical Fragments.* Princeton University Press, 1973, p. 130.

25. Cf. John A. T. Robinson, *The Human Face of God.* Westminster Press, 1973, pp. 156, 186.

26. I am using "messianic secret" as a general term for all the material in Mark which suggests that Jesus' ministry had aspects which were less than public. A more technical discussion would need to make careful distinctions between Jesus' commands to silence, the misunderstanding on the part of his disciples, the theory about the incomprehensibility of the parables, etc. Some of these elements were in the pre-Markan tradition, where they had their own functions, and some are only in the Markan editing. For a full discussion, see the recent volume edited by Christopher Tucket, *The Messianic Secret,* Fortress Press, 1983, an anthology of key essays from several points of view.

27. Differing reconstructions, each of which argue that Mark was working with traditional materials in this section, but understand Mark's editorial work differently, may be found in H. W. Kuhn, Ältere Sammlungen im Markusevangelium, Vandenhoeck & Ruprecht, 1971; and Joanna Dewey, *Markan Public Debate,* Scholars Press, 1980.

28. See T. A. Burkill, *Mysterious Revelation: An Examination of the Meaning of St. Mark's Gospel.* Cornell University Press, 1963, pp. 168-87.

29. Recent studies have shown that some of the secrecy motifs were already in the traditional material which came to Mark. But it was Mark himself who added considerable elements to the secrecy motif and who integrated the whole into a comprehensive secrecy theme which permeates the entire narrative structure. See the essays in Christopher Tucket, *The Messianic Secret,* Fortress Press, 1983.

30. William Wrede, *The Messianic Secret.* James Clarke & Co., 1971. The book was originally published in Germany in 1901.

31. Hans Conzelmann, "Present and Future in the Synoptic Tradition," *Journal for Theology and Church.* Harper & Row, 1968, Vol. V, p. 43.

32. Text from *The Book of Common Prayer of the Protestant Episcopal Church,* as cited in Hugh T. Kerr, *Readings in Christian Thought,* pp. 75-76.

33. Text from *The Creeds of Christendom,* by Phillip Schaff (Harper & Bros., 1932), Vol. II, pp. 62-63, as cited in Kerr, *Readings in Christian Thought,* p. 76.

34. Phillip Wheelwright, *The Burning Fountain.* Indiana University Press, 1954, pp. 70-71.

35. Text from John Dillenberger, *Martin Luther: Selections from His Writings.* Doubleday & Co., 1961, p. 53.

36. See the quotation from Aristotle in J. D. G. Evans, *Aristotle's Concept of Dialectic.* Cambridge University Press, 1977, p. 55. See also Alfred North Whitehead, *Science and the Modern World,* "In formal logic a contradiction is a sign of defeat; but in the evolution of real knowledge it marks the first step in progress toward victory." That is, in this view the value of paradox is that it is a stimulus toward further thought, which can then be expressed in nonparadoxical language.

37. Wheelwright, *Burning Fountain,* p. 71.

38. For a clear discussion of the way formal logic uses these terms, see Irving M. Copi, *Introduction to Logic.* Macmillan, 5th edition, 1978, pp. 165-78.

39. See for example A. J. Ayer, *Language, Truth, and Logic,* Dover Press, 2nd edition, 1952; and A. G. N. Flew and A. MacIntyre, *New Essays in Philosophical Theology,* Macmillan, 1970, and the writings of the early Wittgenstein.

40. Ludwig Wittgenstein, *Philosophical Investigations.* Basil Blackwell, 1953, p. 8.

41. John Macquarrie, *God-Talk: An Examination of the Language and Logic of Theology.* SCM Press, 1967, pp. 123-46.

42. Niebuhr, *Nature and Destiny of Man,* Vol. II, p. 61.

43. Sören Kierkegaard, *Philosophical Fragments.* Princeton University Press, 1941, pp. 194, 290-291. Cf. also pp. 188, 528.

44. Sören Kierkegaard, *Philosophical Fragments.* Princeton University Press, 1936, p. 68.

45. Sören Kierkegaard, *Training in Christianity.* Princeton University Press, 1944, p. 131.

46. Sören Kierkegaard, *Concluding Unscientific Postscript,* p. 187.

47. Richard Braithwaite, *An Empiricist's View of the Nature of Religious Belief,* Cambridge University Press, 1955, as cited in John Hick, ed., *The Existence of God,* Macmillan, 1964, p. 249.

48. Wheelwright, *Burning Fountain,* p. 4.

49. Phillip Wheelwright, *Metaphor and Reality.* Indiana University Press, 1962, p. 162.

50. Ludwig Wittgenstein wrote concerning the bewitching spell which operating with a single picture had over his early work: "A picture held us captive. And we could not get outside it"(*Philosophical Investigations,* §115). Anthony Thiselton

comments on this: "What misleads us is not simply the power of a model or metaphor as such, but the fact that all too often one way of seeing a particular problem is wholly dictated by a single controlling picture which excludes all others. In these circumstances it exercises a spell over us, which bewitches our intelligence and blinds us to other ways of seeing. . . ." *The Two Horizons: New Testament Hermeneutic and Philosophical Description.* Eerdmans, 1980, p. 432.

51. This is because the concern of the church fathers was never ontology or metaphysics per se but *salvation.* Christ had to be fully divine because only a divine being could save (Athanasius at Nicea). And he had to be truly human because "that which Christ has not assumed he cannot heal" (the Cappadocian fathers at Chalcedon).I am indebted to Professor Susan Schreiner for this clarification.

52. See Franz Jozef van Beeck, S. J. *Christ Proclaimed: Christology as Rhetoric.* Paulist Press, 1979, especially pp. 130-34.

53. Wheelwright, *Metaphor and Reality,* pp. 45-46.

54. For a description of the process of "infinite qualification" by which religious language functions, see Ian T. Ramsey, *Religious Language.* Macmillan, 1967, pp. 68-102.

55. Sheldon B. Kopp, *If You Meet the Buddha on the Road, Kill Him.* SBB Press, 1972.

56. See Wheelwright, *Metaphor and Reality,* p. 22, and *Burning Fountain,* p. 269, who gives alternate translations for what is literally "The Tao which can be *tao*-ed is not the real Tao."

57. Ludwig Wittgenstein, *Tractatus Logico-philosophicus.* Kegan Paul, 1922, p. 189.

58. Thomas McPherson, "Religion as the Inexpressible" in *New Essays in Philosophical Theology,* ed. Anthony Flew and Alasdair MacIntyre. SCM Press, 1955, p. 133.

59. In my opinion this is the most positive interpretation that can be placed on the contemporary practice of glossalalia. Cf. the German charismatic pastor A. Bittlinger's essay, "Der neutestamentliche charismatische Gottesdienst im Lichte der heutigen charismatischen Erneuerung der Kirche" in J. Panagopoulos, ed., *Prophetic Vocation in the New Testament and Today,* Brill, 1977, pp. 186-209.

60. Cf. Robert W. Funk, *Language, Hermeneutic, and Word of God,* Harper & Row, 1966; and *Parables and Presence,* Fortress Press, 1982; John Dominic Crossan, *In Parables: The Challenge of the Historical Jesus,* Harper & Row, 1973; *The Dark Interval: Toward a Theology of Story,* Argus Communications, 1975; *Cliffs of Fall: Paradox and Polyvalence in the Parables of Jesus,* Seabury Press, 1980.

61. The phrase is from Gerhard Ebeling, as cited in Robert Funk, *Language, Hermeneutic, and Word of God,* p. 129.

62. For many other examples of the paradoxical language of Hinduism and Buddhism, see W. T. Stace, *Mysticism and Philosophy,* Humanities Press, 1969, Chapter IV. Also R. H. L. Slater, *Paradox and Nirvana.* University of Chicago Press, 1951.

63. John Dominic Crossan, "Biblical Truth as Dialectical Analysis," in *Chicago Studies* VI (March 1967), p. 297.

64. Ian Barbour, *Issues in Science and Religion,* Harper & Row (1971), pp. 279-82, gives a clear description, in nontechnical language, of such experiments.

65. *Ibid.,* p. 283.

66. John Gardner, *Sunlight Dialogues.* Ballantine, 1982. Other examples are William Faulkner, *The Sound and the Fury.* Random House, 1954; *Absalom, Absalom.* Random House, 1972.

67. Cf. Sören Kierkegaard, *Works of Love*. Harper & Row, 1964, pp. 10-11, 23-33.

68. See Ian Ramsey, *Religious Language,* 38-39, on the "logically odd" character of the language of love.

69. Gilbert Ryle, *Dilemmas*. Cambridge University Press, 1954, pp. 111-29. "Formal" and "informal" in this connection, be it noted, have to do with form and content. "Formal" logic is concerned with form alone, not with content. "Informal" logic does not mean "relaxed, less rigid" but means the logic is influenced by the content with which it deals, and is not determined by forms alone.

70. *Ibid.,* pp. 118-19.

71. Cf. Wheelwright, *Burning Fountain,* pp. 8-16. Discussing the borderline I-and-the-world, Wheelwright rejects both the attempt to reduce "I" to "the world" (of matter), and the attempts to reduce matter to the knowing "I" (idealism). "Both materialist and idealist can make a strong case for their respective positions, but only by a willingness to belittle half the evidence. Each of them backs a single kind of insight to the limit, believing consistency of interpretation to be more important than fulness of reference. Their contrasting positions can be made to look logical, but they are not humanly reasonable. . . . Better a reasonable paradox than a cantankerously one-sided syllogism" (*Burning Fountain,* pp. 11-12).

72. Ramsey, *Religious Language,* pp. 53, 102, 215.

73. The phrase is from F. Waismann, quoted by the editor in *New Essays in Religious Language,* ed. Dallas High, Oxford University Press, 1969, p. xii. It was the *early* Wittgenstein who argued that what can be said at all can be said clearly, a principle he later qualified. But there is such a thing as being *clear* about why we need vague words and constructions in order to communicate. Cf. Mark Platts's discussion of the "paradoxes" (in the popular sense) involved in such expressions as "That's a heap of sand." How many grains make a "heap"? Can I ever get a "heap" of sand by adding one grain at a time and asking each time, "Is it a heap now?" Such language is imprecise and unclear, yet we cannot and should not get by without it. Mark Platts, *Ways of Meaning*. Routledge and Kegan Paul, 1979, pp. 217-26.

74. Rudolf Bultmann, *Theology of the New Testament*. II, p. 128.

75. Cf. John Hick, "Religious Statements as Factually Significant" in John Hick, ed., *The Existence of God*. Macmillan, 1964, pp. 260-61.

76. Gilbert Ryle, "Philosophical Arguments," in A. J. Ayer, ed., *Logical Positivism*. The Free Press, 1959, pp. 330-336.

77. Ronald Hepburn, *Christianity and Paradox: Critical Studies in Twentieth-Century Theology*. Pegasus, 1968, p. 1.

78. This phrase is usually attributed to Tertullian, but cannot be found in his writings. Tertullian says *"ineptum"* and *"impossibile"* instead of *"absurdum."* The phrase is, however, a fair enough summary of some aspects of Tertullian's work.

79. As cited in Wolfhart Pannenberg, *Basic Questions in Theology*. Fortress Press, 1971, p. 48. By "reason" Luther usually meant something like "common sense," which tells us that good works make us acceptable before God.

80. Sören Kierkegaard, as cited by William Barrett, *Irrational Man: A Study in Existential Philosophy*. Doubleday, 1958, p. 149.

81. Karl Barth, *The Epistle to the Romans*. Oxford University Press, 1933, pp. 143-44.

82. Edward Schillebeeckx, *The Understanding of Faith,* Seabury, 1972, pp. 35-36, argues that theology too must abide by the universal laws of logic, that it cannot plead for a suspension of logic or a special kind of logic, but that this only means that religious language, including paradox, must be *able to give account of itself* in logical terms. A similar argument is made by Wolfhart Pannenberg, *Jesus: God and*

139

Man, SCM Press, 1968, p. 157; and Hans Küng, *On Being a Christian,* Doubleday, 1976, pp. 87, 350-51, 448-50.

83. See Ernst Nagel, "Logic Without Ontology" in *Naturalism and the Human Spirit,* ed. Y. H. Krikarian, Columbia University Press, 1944; and Irving M. Copi and James A. Gould, eds., *Contemporary Philosophical Logic,* St. Martin's Press, 1978, Part IV, "Logic and Ontology."

84. Copi, *Introduction to Logic,* fifth edition, 366-69.

85. For a collection of essays illustrating the variety within the field of logic, see Peter T. Manicas, ed., *Logic as Philosophy: An Introductory Anthology,* Van Nostrand Reinhold Co., 1971; and Copi and Gould, *Contemporary Philosophical Logic.* For a recent discussion of newly developed logical systems which are able to embrace inconsistency, see Nicholas Rescher and Robert Brandon, *The Logic of Inconsistency,* Blackwell, 1980.

86. S. I. Hayakawa, *Language in Thought and Action.* Harcourt, Brace, & Co., 1949, p. 240.

87. George Boas, *The Limits of Reason.* Harper & Row, 1961, p. 20.

88. Copi, *Introduction to Logic,* p. 321.

89. See Pannenberg, *Jesus: God and Man,* p. 184; Ramsey, *Religious Language,* pp. 196-99; and especially van Beeck, *Christology as Rhetoric,* p. 128.